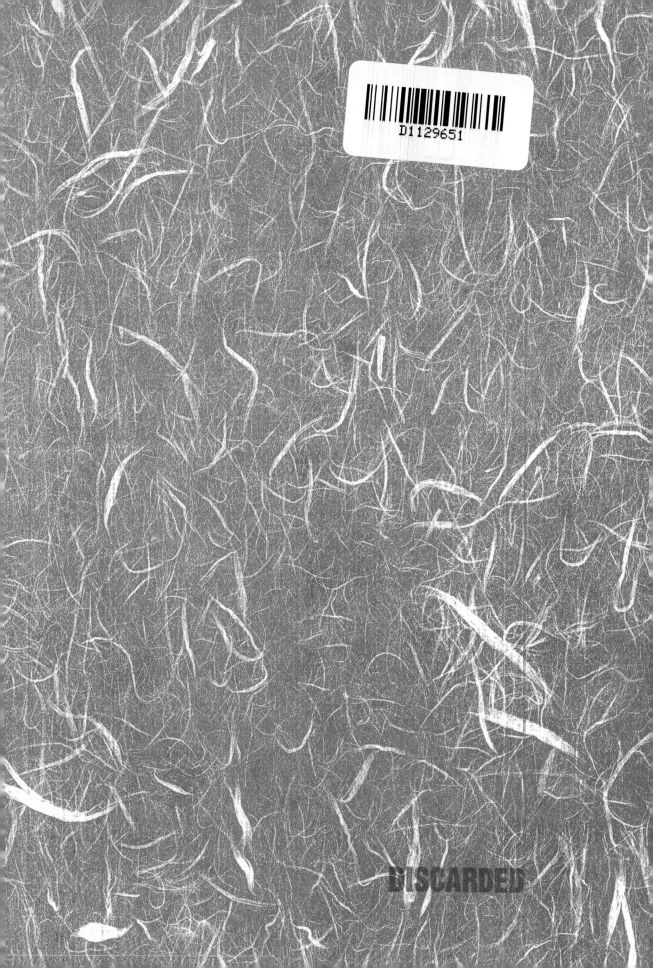

The Temples of Kyoto

The Temples of Kyoto

Text by **Donald Richie**
Photographs by **Alexandre Georges**

Charles E. Tuttle Company
Rutland, Vermont & Tokyo, Japan

The photographs on pp. 45, 71, 74
were taken by Donald Richie.

Published by the
Charles E. Tuttle Company, Inc. of
Rutland, Vermont & Tokyo, Japan
with editorial offices at
2-6 Suido 1-chome, Bunkyo-ku,
Tokyo 112

LCC Card No. 94-62021
ISBN 0-8048-2032-5

First edition, 1995

Printed in Singapore

for

Katherine Wells

Contents

Commit neither the error of the naive reader, who is depressed by massacres and legal tortures and who congratulates himself upon living in the twentieth century, nor that of the reader of historical novels, who safely delights in the splendid crimes and scandals of the past—above all, let us not envy the past its stability . . .

"Ah, Mon Beau Château . . . "
—MARGUERITE YOURCENAR

Preface

京都の寺

There are nearly two thousand places of worship in Kyoto and the great majority of them are Buddhist temples. Any book can thus hold only a certain number. This one includes twenty-one, yet in a sense it also contains them all. Neither a history nor a guide, it is an illustrated essay on the nature and the history of the Buddhist temple. It could thus have included less, or more, or those different from the ones chosen.

That choice was determined years before the text was written when the photographer, in the city for the first time, turned his trained architectural eye only upon what interested him. Consequently, many a famous temple is not included and some included are not famous at all. Further, since it was the design, the space of the place which appealed, no distinction was made as to just which part of the space was being rendered. The eccentric result is a portfolio of pictures which attempts to render no precise information and at the same time truly captures the presence of the temples of Kyoto.

These construct a spatial narrative—a sheaf of vistas which define but do not limit. In this way the photographer is very like the *bunjin* artists of old Japan, those profound amateurs who looked for essence, not in order, but in the sighting of a scene.

In the same fashion, the author, almost equally ignorant, years later following the path of the photographer he never met, has attempted to do with time what had been done with space—to make a temporal record of what he has read or heard or himself seen.

So, I wanted something like a narrative—a broken chronology with many a hole through which one might peer back into time itself, a history arranged

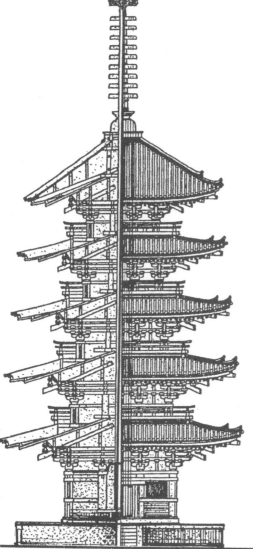

in layers through which we can move from one temple to the next.

Together, the text and pictures seek then to define the temple. The photos contain few people and the text is filled with the deeds of the dead. A kind of definition seems possible.

—DONALD RICHIE

Introduction

京都の寺

 A city of temples reminds one of some lost vision of a moral order—where the manlike god lives in his holy house and all is eternity. Seen from a distance, these temple-cities—Benares, the Katmandu valley towns, Kyoto—still offer this view. The stupa or the *to* against the new winter dawn seems to hold out a vision of some holy metropolis from where we have come and toward which we returning.

Yet these celestial-seeming cities are nonetheless the work of man and they are of the same common earth that we are—that dappled soil of hopes and fears, of a self never wholly outside, yet never entirely in.

Such holy cities, like all the others, are thus also worldly, venal: as elsewhere the making of the money accommodates the lust for power. Unlike the prosaic secular city, however, these municipalities of temples have their saving concern. No matter how religion is perverted in its politicization, it still rests upon an individual vision, a need, a hope. In the grandest of the imperial temples where all is tradition, ritual, the accumulation of land and the avoidance of taxes, there is still somewhere, in some corner, a man kneeling, trying to both lose and find himself.

卍

Buddhism came to Japan on October 13, in the thirteenth year of the reign of the emperor Kimmei—that is, 552. This is recorded in the *Nihongi,* that government-commissioned chronological history which appeared two hundred years later in 720 but was still accepted as accurate.

The reason that the date is so precisely known is that this is the day that a Korean envoy presented to the Japanese court a gold-plated Buddha, a gift from his king, Song-myong of the Paekche. Along with it came a letter in which Buddhism was highly praised, something of its history was imparted—its beginnings in India and its travels through China—the missal concluding with the information that the Buddha himself had said that his teachings would travel east.

Kimmei, emperor of this land furthest east, is said to have been both pleased and impressed, stating that he had never seen anything more beautiful than the face on this statue of the Buddha. Of a mind to import the religion into his own land, the emperor held a council. One minister said that since it had been accepted elsewhere it ought to be accepted here as well. Another, however, said that this would be dangerous. From times past it was the native gods—those later to be identified as Shinto—who had protected the land. Introducing such competition would make them angry.

Since neither of the ministers would back down and since no agreement seemed possible, Kimmei then did something we would now find very Japanese. He decided that both religions would be observed—that of the native gods and that of the new one. This pragmatic solution caused some initial difficulty but it has worn well. Shinto and Buddhism remain the two religions of the Japanese. The first is observed by the newly born, by those reaching the ages of three, five, and seven, and those getting married; the second is officially the province of the dying and the dead.

卍

Buddhism was already at least a thousand years old when it came to Japan. During this time the religion had much changed shape. It had become a complex set of doctrinal beliefs far from the tenets of its founder.

Originally the Buddha had taught that the release from this period of suffering called life could be achieved through enlightenment—by following the prescribed commandments making up the eightfold path. These were of a simplicity and universality that remind of Jesus' later advice. One was to follow the right view with the right intention as expressed in right speech and demonstrated in the right action, which would lead to the right livelihood, as achieved through right effort, right mindedness, and right concentration.

Prescriptions this artless call for interpretation and over the years the eightfold path became littered with them. They multiplied until eventually, five hundred years after the death of the historical Buddha, the overburdened belief broke into two—a major schism had occurred.

A large number of priests began to preach that traditional teachings had left behind the true intentions of the Buddha. The religion had come to imply that only those with special capacities—such as intelligence and perseverance—could hope to correctly follow the eightfold path. Actually, they said, the Buddha did not intend anything like this. On his deathbed, these priests maintained, he had revealed that anyone—and this included everyone—had the potential for Buddhahood.

Those who claimed this called their Buddhism the Greater Vehicle (Mahayana). They could then call their conservative rivals the Lesser Vehicle (Hinayana). This schism—still observed—provided endless fuel for quarrels and much complicated the role of the religion in Japan.

Buddhism was exclusively of neither camp. Then as now, the recent import was carefully sorted over and only those elements attractive to the new believers were incorporated. Early Japanese Buddhism is thus a pragmatic amalgam of both Mahayanan and Hinayanan Buddhism.

Nonetheless, much of the spirit of strife occasioned by the original schism remained to trouble the Buddhist church in Japan, though many of the benefits of a much larger number of aristocratic and moneyed believers continued to ornament and enrich the church.

A Mahayanan idea which took deep root in Japan was that the Buddha was a transcendent being. Leaving behind his mortal form, he ascended to the heavens and there reigned, welcoming all true believers. If he was deity, and no longer of this world, however, then someone to intercede was necessary.

Christianity at this point found Jesus Christ. Buddhism discovered the bodhisattva, the Buddha-to-be, a kind of messenger, though of much greater standing, a being who, though meeting all the requirements for Buddhahood, in great compassion postponed entry in order to help those left behind also achieve this desired state.

This Buddha himself took three bodhisattva-like forms. He was to be seen as the healing Buddha (called Yakushi in Japan), the Buddha of enlightenment (Amida) and the Buddha of the future (Miroku). In this way, also, Mahayana believers could begin to account for the entire pantheon of Buddhas and other supernatural beings it had appropriated from Hinayanan belief as well as from

Hinduism and other local religions. These could be attached to appropriate forms of the Buddha-bodhisattva and thus create a semblance of order.

It was order which appealed to the seventh-century rulers of Japan. The government was but loosely organized, the religion was an uneasy amalgam of beliefs both native and important. Already the example of civilized China was inspiring the Japanese, and thus the fact that Buddhism was perceived as Chinese made it all the more welcome in Japan.

Just as Japan was to so spectacularly learn later from Europe and America, it now begin to practice that combination of appropriation and internalization common to all countries but perhaps perfected in this one. Pursuing its new aims, Japan sent four missions to Sui China (859–618) from 600 to 614, and from 630 to 838 many more to the Tang—that great Chinese dynasty (618–907) the influence of which was to have such a decisive effect on Japan.

These missions brought back not only Buddhist but also Confucian ideas. In 604 when the regent, Prince Shotoku, formulated his famous constitution—five years earlier than the like-minded Mohammed who, on the other side of the world, was also to proclaim a new state: Islam—he not only called for reverence for Buddhism but also insisted upon Confucian principles: ministers should obey imperial commands, harmony should be prized, and so on.

By 645 when the Taika (Great Change) Reforms were instituted, it was the Tang pattern which was utilized and the Japanese state was recast in the Chinese model. Just as the country was to later revolutionize itself in its nineteenth-century efforts to "catch up with the West," so it now remade its institutions as it caught up with the Tang. The ideal was a centralized and bureaucratic state. There was even a redistribution of land—something which would not again occur until 1945. In theory everyone got the same amount. Actually, some got more than others and within a century Buddhist temples, Shinto shrines, and aristocratic families had all accumulated private estates.

The Tang pattern was secured when the Taiho (Great Treasure) Code was promulgated in 702. It gave Japan a symmetrical and elaborate bureaucratic structure—one which, in one form or another, still works today. With this as a base, bit by bit anything deemed useful was imported from the Tang and its

Korean conduit into Japan: the language, the architecture, new ways of drawing, sculpting, and under it all, an accepted and basic Buddhist system of beliefs.

This was mainly of the Mahayana persuasion, though an animosity toward the Hinayana belief was not at first apparent. Rather some sort of powerful amalgam was sought, found, and referred to as the "highest absolute." United, this expansive version of Buddhist doctrine saw to it that temples and priests proliferated, and that the influence of the Buddhist church grew.

卐

The city of Kyoto was the capital of Japan and home of the imperial court from 794 to 1868. It was consequently not only the cradle of this newly Sinoized civilization but also the keeper of its culture.

The city remains a treasure house—literally: it possesses a total of 202 National Treasures (20 percent of the country's total) and 1,596 Important Cultural Assets (15 percent of that total). It also contains many of the finest examples of Buddhist architecture in the country, well over 1500 temples.

Odd, this last, because the city was originally built to get away from Buddhist influence.

The reason for the intended avoidance was that ever since this religion had been introduced into the country its influence had been growing—some thought unduly. This was because Buddhism, like most religions, offered an array of class opportunities which proved amenable to the already Sinoized imperial court.

Just as the Chinese propensity for hierarchical order had provided a model to the Japanese government—a system of court ranks suitable to an aristocratic society was already built into it—so, too, the Buddhist religion proved itself friendly to a similar stratification and could further be used to support the newly consolidated power, centered as it was upon an imperial house and a regent family.

What became known as Nara Buddhism consisted of six schools: Sanron, Hosso, Kegon, Jojitsu, Kusha, and Ritsu. The first three belonged to the Mahayana tradition, the last three to the Hinayana and they thus offered the priests a survey of contemporary Buddhist thought. (Three of them still exist: Hosso at Kofuku-ji and Yakushi-ji, Kegon at Todai-ji, and Ritsu at Toshodaiji.) Besides learned study the priests' only other duty was to perform rituals for the government—these were to assure the security of the state and to offer aristocratic patrons efficacious prayers

It was the court which was Buddhist. The imperial family and the influential noble houses were the true believers and held the monopoly on the new religion—it was not until much later (around 1200) that Buddhism became in any sense a popular religion.

This is different from the pattern observed in other major religions: Christianity began among what we would now call the underprivileged and then spread upward; the Muslim religion too was initially a popular belief. But in Japan most new institutions follow a different pattern: they are initially appropriated by whatever passes for aristocracy and are only then passed on to the lower echelons.

One of the attributes of Japanese Buddhism (in contrast with Buddhism elsewhere) is this tie with the state. The government patronized and thus controlled Buddhist organizations, while they—in return as it were—gave it spiritual and moral support, even though this often meant a compromise of churchly principles.

The ruling house took early to Buddhism. Just a generation after the death of Prince Shotoku, who had introduced the religion, the emperor Kotoku became so Buddhist that he ordered the destruction of the groves belonging to the Ikukunitama Shrine and is remembered in the *Nihongi* as having honored Buddhism and despised Shinto.

The later emperor Shomu was already early endorsing the fashionable new belief. He had by 742 piously announced a system of national temples, the Kokubun-ji, which linked the propagation of faith with the consolidation of state power. This he established in 752 with ceremonies at Todai-ji in Nara— then capital of the country.

The event was the inauguration of the Great Buddha, a bronze statue fifty-three feet in height—the cosmic Buddha Vairocana (*Daibutsu* or "Great Buddha" in Japanese)—an undertaking so extreme that it used up all the copper in the country and required eight attempts before it was successfully cast.

Housed in the new main hall of Todai-ji, the largest wooden building in the world, the statue was the figurehead of state religious ambitions. There was nothing this big in all of Tang China and so it called for inauguration ceremonies much more lavish than usual. Priests and royal envoys from as far away as Persia attended—ten thousand in all—and a high-ranking cleric all the way from India was there to paint in the pupils of the statue's eyes and give it symbolic life. The spectacle—for it was the grandest occasion in Japan so far— was memorable.

Memorable too was the new power that this gave the church. The court thought that it would be strengthened by an affiliation with the Buddhist church. It had perhaps not occurred to it that the church would be the more strengthened by this affiliation with the civil government.

The imperial house itself was thus eventually challenged by the growing power of the church. An example was the Buddhist priest Dokyo, who boldly attempted to influence the throne. The empress Koken, daughter of the emperor Shomu, was in retirement when she came under this priestly influence. Whether due to Buddhist invigoration or not, she emerged from retirement, became the empress Shotoku, and then elevated Dokyo to a much higher position, that of *dajodaijin-zenji,* priest-premier.

The power of Buddhism was much deplored, earlier instances of imperial ladies falling under the spell of priests were cited, and a popular poem of the period commemorated these scandalous events with its verses about hammers of power lying beneath priestly robes.

卍

Escaping these dangerous Buddhist influences was among several reasons, then, that the emperor Kammu in 784, only three years on the throne, had the old capital moved from Nara to Nagaoka. He then, ten years later, had it installed in its present location (then Heian-kyo, now Kyoto). He thus remedied his problem in what we now recognize as a Japanese manner— rather than remove the monks he removed the city.

He had his geomancers seek out a proper site: mountains to the north, plains to the south, a river running through it; he notified the tutelary deity of the Kamo Shrine and the Sun Goddess at Ise of the change of address; sent messengers to the tombs of all the emperors from three generations back, and then had the major buildings (the palace, the temple) knocked down and transported to the new site five miles away. There he gave his new city a

卍 ──

hopeful new name—Capital of Peace and Tranquillity—and, as though to assure this, among its many specifications was one restricting the building of temples within the boundaries of this new capital.

Finished, Heian-kyo was by eighth-century standards enormous. It measured three miles east to west and three and a half miles north to south. The boundaries were rectangular and great avenues crossed each other at regular intervals. One such divided the city into east and west (or left and right) capitals. It was nearly three hundred feet wide making it quite the widest avenue in the world. At its head stood the palace enclosure, the northern side of which formed part of the city limits; it measured one mile by three-quarters of a mile, and had fourteen gates.

It was a smaller version of the Tang dynasty capital of Chang'an (modern Xi'an), the same city which had also served as earlier inspiration for Nara—but, of course, now without the many temples. Kammu carefully limited both their number and the admission of their priests.

Inside the city limits only two temples were permitted. Much smaller than any in Nara, they were given small plots symmetrically left and right of the main avenue. The western temple, Sai-ji, had so little support that it shortly withered. The eastern, To-ji, survived only because it formed a main branch of the Shingon sect in 835. Even now the temple is, in more senses than one, on the wrong side of the tracks.

Yet, even as anti-Buddhist edicts were promulgated, temples were rising and priests were joining. Outside the city walls it seemed like a sudden religious revival though it was in fact a scramble to get tax-free estates—a loophole which Kammu had left unplugged. A later imperial edict, admitting the difficulty, read: "If this continues, shortly there will be no land which is not temple property."

A further problem was that the court itself was already so permeated with Buddhism that the sometimes baleful ecclesiastical influence was all but impossible to eradicate. The problem was familiar one. Two parallel systems of power always quarrel: the church and the state have never anywhere been amicable.

A partial solution lay in deciding that it was *Nara* Buddhism which was the enemy and not Buddhism itself. A solution should be possible if only a new kind of Buddhism could be found—one without dangerous political ambitions. An accommodation was necessary. Consequently, not one but two such examples of benign Buddhism were shortly located.

The monks Saicho (767–822) and Kukai (774–835) had joined a trading mission in 804 and gone to China. Each brought back a separate set of Buddhist tantric beliefs. Saicho returned and consolidated the Tendai (T'ien-t'ai) sect, and its eventual headquarters at Enryaku-ji on Mount Hiei above Heian-kyo. Kukai founded the Shingon sect and set himself up at To-ji in the southern section of the capital and over at Ishiyama-dera, on the other side of Mount Hiei. He also later founded Kongobu-ji on Mount Koya. There, under his posthumous canonical name, Kobo Daishi, he lives still. Visitors are shown the moss-covered temple in which he lies, not dead, but meditating, awaiting the coming of the Buddha of the future.

This being will, among his other duties, have to purify his religion. Buddhism held that the state must reflect the order of the universe and that this is hierarchical, everything emanating from the permanent center. It could thus be used to justify the political centralization of the country. Buddhism in Japan—of the Nara variety or otherwise—had from the first been in this sense worldly. So are, to be sure, most religions, but the forms which Japanese Buddhism took made it seem even more so.

卍

The Buddhist temple was everywhere (and at the same time more than) a place devoted to worship of the Buddha. It functioned as a residence for monks and nuns, where they studied the sutras and trained in ascetic practices, and it was in addition a place for lay worshippers to gather. There was thus—from the first, in all temples, in all Buddhist countries—a social element. It was the degree of this which differed in Japan.

The etymology of the Japanese term for temple, *tera*, suggests a predominance of the idea of place. The word derives from the Pali word *thera,* which means "elders," indicating perhaps a place where the church elders lived. The characters used are from the pre-Buddhist Han dynasty and indicate an area where bureaucratic officers stay, a reference to Confucian laws and their implementation. Thus, the predominantly social nature of later temples is suggested in the term.

This is not invariably so in other religions. The etymology of the English "temple," for example, suggests less worldly concerns. It is from the Latin *templum* which means a space measured out for sanctuary—thus containing a nuance missing in the Japanese.

Bruno Taut, the first serious foreign student of Japanese architecture, at once recognized that "temples constitute no clearly delimited space, as do churches, for instance, in the West . . . ." He was puzzled by this and only began to understand when a Japanese architect friend informed him that temples were originally mostly people's houses—the statues and altars had just been added: Buddha had moved in and stayed.

This domestic Buddhism was necessary in that it supplied what the native religion, Shinto (which Taut did not consider a religion at all) did not. With Buddhism came accommodation, structure, and reason.

卐

It followed then that Buddhist temples were patterned in part after social and political desires—just what one might expect from a religion which was in Japan initially so close to the needs of the state.

In this Japanese temples were unlike both Shinto shrines—where a closeness to divine nature is insisted upon by the architecture itself—and Western churches, where the aspiring nature of Christianity is made visible in striving cathedral towers and lofty naves.

Japanese Buddhist architecture followed functional needs—practical, spiritual, and social. By the eighth century a temple pattern had evolved. Called the *shichido garan* (seven-halled temple), it typically consisted of: the pagoda (*to*), a multistoried tower where relics such as nominal remains of the Buddha were enshrined; the main or "Buddha" hall (*kondo*, literally "golden hall,") wherein was housed the principal object of worship; the lecture hall (*kodo*), usually the largest structure in the compound—where monks or nuns gathered for instruction, study, or ritual; the drum or bell tower (*koro*); the sutra repository (*kyozo*); the dormitories (*sobo*); and the dining hall (*jikido*).

There were other buildings as well. These included the inner sanctuary (*naijin*) where the priests performed their rituals, the outer sanctuary (*gaijin*) where laymen worshipped, bathrooms, toilets, and the various gates. These last were grouped into the outer gates (*daimon*) which were named after the cardinal points. The south gate (*nan-daimon*) was the front or main gate. The inner or middle gate (*chumon*) opened into the main precincts which contained the pagoda and the main hall. Later developments included the massive *sanmon* (triple gate) of Zen found in temples such as Tofuku-ji, Nanzen-ji, and the Chion-in. Balanced, symmetrical, speaking of order in a Chinese accent, this early architecture also displayed direct authority. It was a spatial narrative form, an architectural text which from its inception indicated a secular society and the need for a man-made order.

卍

In this the imported Buddhist temple was as different from the local Shinto shrine as were the two religions from each other.

Buddhism in all of its forms encourages thoughts of evanescence, transience, the passing of all things, the attractions of the next world. It is also universalist and moralistic. Shinto—the native animistic religion of Japan—is vital: concerned only with the here and now. It is both pluralistic and amoral. It is also phobic about pollution and decay, while Buddhism is morbid in its reflections upon the imminence of death.

It was through fears of death and hopes of the consequent life beyond that Buddhism achieved its popularity—unlike Shinto which could threaten or promise nothing of the sort. Buddhism consequently achieved a political power which Shinto could never match.

At the same time, however, different though the two religions appeared, they were—such being the way of the country—shortly brought into a kind of harmony with each other. Indeed, the ease with which these apparently inimical beliefs were accommodated makes one wonder about the real depth of either.

Sir George Sansom has voiced these doubts. "The Japanese as a people have displayed in matters of belief a tolerance amounting almost to indifference." But there was also undoubtedly another reason for this religious alloy, one which Karel van Wolferen has indicated in speaking of the melding of Shinto with Buddhism: "An amalgamation of the two religions was clearly an official policy designed to strengthen their joint endorsement of existing worldly rule."

Of the process itself, Shuichi Kato has written that "Buddhism in Japan absorbed native gods and was simultaneously transformed by contact with them . . . the Japanese gods themselves were transformed by Buddhism, since gods who once were objects of worship prior to the arrival of Buddhism did not have their own myths, doctrines, shrines, or images."

Later, "under the influence of Buddhism, consistent myths and doctrines were created, the architecture of Shinto shrines was developed, and images of gods were produced." The popular Shinto deity Hachiman is called Hachiman Daibosatsu, and his original home is described as the Pure Land in the west where he is otherwise known as Amida. Amaterasu Omikami, the Sun Goddess, is also at holy Ise known as the Kanzeon Bosatsu, that is, as the incarnation of the Bodhisattva Avalokiteshvara.

There was a name for this: *honji suijaku,* which means the manifestation of the Buddha incarnated in the form of the native gods. In taking over Shinto to this extent Buddhist authorities knew what they were doing since the native religion still defined the natives. It still continues to do so, for as Nicholas Palevsky has written: "Shinto is characterized not by scriptures and churches but by . . . a concern for purity and defilement . . . Shinto is not so much a matter of personal belief as it is of being Japanese."

卐

Beneath the Chinese infatuation (as beneath later crushes on things European and American) this native inclination persists. It resisted the ethical high-mindedness which so reflected the philosophy of Confucious, it opposed the presumed universality of China with the concrete detail and the specific example; to the model conduct of the sages, it opposed the beauty and variety of the world it knew.

No matter how much the eighth-century aristocrat was convinced of China's greatness, he is unlikely to have consequently altered all of his feelings and changed all of his opinions. Just as the modern Japanese resists a complete Westernization (one does not trod shod in the house, one does not lather in the bath), so his ancestor must have resisted a complete Sinozation.

There is an indication of this in a complaint seen in a 724 Nara report which said that the capital lacked majesty and virtue because there were so many native plank-roofed dwellings and thatched roofs. These are difficult to build and easy to destroy, yet their presence was persisting. The report advised that all high-ranking persons be required to erect tiled dwellings and to paint them red and white in the Chinese style.

Native Japanese needs and tastes continued, however, to assert themselves and often accounted for the combinations through which the foreign influence was changed into something which was both more practical and more in accord with being Japanese.

An architectural example is that important part of the temple known as the *kondo,* or Buddha hall. The Japanese originally saw it in the form of a scaled model brought by a Paekche mission in 588. The first such halls constructed in Japan were all careful copies. Eventually these were seen as impractical.

The completely symmetrical is something rarely seen in native Japanese art—it too often sacrifices human convenience for reasons both aesthetic and symbolic. The Chinese-style *kondo* symmetrically dispensed with practicality for symmetry and comfort for effect. Simple human convenience, always prized in Japan, was consequently sacrificed. So, the hall was soon after adapted to native purposes which attempted to retain something of Chinese dignity while accommodating Japanese pragmatic needs. Now the new Buddha hall could hold a lay congregation indoors where they could see and hear the service, and at the same time it had space in which to perform the tantric rites in secrecy.

In this manner an approximation of a national style was returned to religious architecture. It shared with Shinto a practicality, a directness, a humanity one might say, which the Chinese original had not originally evidenced. Now, composed of old and new, the native and the imported, the Buddha hall became Japanese.

卍

Buddhism in Japan was influenced not only by Shinto but also by two systems of thought which, if not precisely religions, functioned remarkably like them. Temple organization and architecture in Japan were in part formed by both Confucianism and Taoism. The former allowed and excused power and the latter extended this power into the further realms of superstition.

They came together in (as seen in one example of their manifestations) geomancy (*hoigaku*). This originally came from China (*fengshui*) and entered

Japan within a decade (554) of Buddhism. It is a complicated technique for the handling (and creating) of good fortune. Taoist in origin, it was taken over only in part in Japan where it became largely a preventative art, one governed by fear of misfortune.

Temporally, it concerns itself not so much with "good days" (for weddings, the beginning of businesses, etc.) as it is with "bad days" when any kind of action was impermissible. Court lady Sei Shonagon (968–1024) has left a despairing account of the exhausting detours necessary on inauspicious occasions and figuring largely in the list of things hateful in her pillow book, the *Makura no Soshi,* are the inconveniences of geomanistic superstition.

Spatially, in equally negative manner, *hoigaku* also concerned itself with things forbidden. Early Buddhist compounds were all built according to forbidding principles. Charts were drawn up with the cardinal points indicated. Here a gate could let in only melancholy; a well in this spot brings worries but a gate does no harm; here, however, a lavatory promises ruin. Such beliefs much affected the lives of the inhabitants.

There was, for example, the belief that evil comes from the northeast. Confucious had slept with his head in that direction and so, consequently did a number of Japanese emperors. Shirakawa, insisted upon it, saying that by lying on his right side with his head to the northeast he could then emulate Buddha's posture as he entered Nirvana. But was this safe, someone wondered and someone else remarked that the great Ise Shrine lay to the south and questioned whether it were proper for the imperial highness to sleep with his feet toward the great shrine. No answer is recorded, but a decision was early reached to avoid the north. Sei Shonagon had included in her listing of Things that People Despise: "The north side of the house."

These geographical ordinances are in some sense still fundamental to Japanese architecture. For example, in any domestic building, on no account should the lavatory, the entrance, or the kitchen be placed on a northeast-southwest axis. The northeast is thought the home of evil and the southwest its compliment. It might be said that there was some original practical reason for this. Southwest winds would tend to fan flames from the kitchen. Whatever—in Japan such reason was not consulted and the Chinese rules were observed.

They still are. Even in a new house, the lavatory is found next to the entryway (and the living room) because this is one way to avoid the dreaded northeast–southwest axis. Even today the home architect consults the architectural soothsayer, who has been known to later sell amulets for points not in order. Even now many buildings in Kyoto (including the imperial palace) have their northeast corners cut off to deflect evil. But before we make too merry over this exhibition of superstitious ignorance it would be well to count the number of hotels in the West which (in by far the preponderance of cases) have no thirteenth floor.

One of the results of geomancy was that the northeast became the dangerous direction in general as well as in particular. The great militant monasteries on Mount Hiei were originally built on those heights because they are northeast of the capital, the palace, and the emperor, and could thus (in theory) protect them.

It is with one of these that the story of the Japanese temple begins.

The

TEMPLES

of

KYOTO

Enryaku-ji

On the heights of Mount Hiei, northeast of Kyoto, sits the ecclesiastical city of Enryaku-ji, headquarters of the Tendai sect and a center for religious meditation, political indoctrination, and warfare since the Heian period (784–1185).

Most of the founders of the major Buddhist sects rising during the following several centuries studied there: Honen of the Jodo sect; Shinran of the Jodo Shin sect; Eisai who introduced the Rinzai Zen sect to Japan; Dogen, who did the same for the Soto sect; Ippen of the Ji sect of Jodo; Kuya of his own Tendai sect; and Nichiren, who founded Nichiren Buddhism—all were trained there.

Enryaku-ji grew as enormous as it was important. Though less than a twentieth of its former size, the temple is still one of the largest in Japan. It now faces Lake Biwa and not Kyoto, the old capital, but is still so big that only a third is readily visitable—in winter the roads to the two other main sections are closed and no buses run.

Originally, however, it was but a collection of mountain huts. These followed only the irregularity of their terrain. In such sites as this the formal Chinese layout was impossible—so was any sustained balance or symmetry. Thus in their very appearance the temples of the new religion constituted a rebuke to the luxurious compounds down on the plain. This is something which the Tendai founder, Saicho (later known as Dengyo Daishi) reinforced in his deathbed message. He advised a "cheerful poverty" on his followers, and thus implied a criticism of those soft and luxurious Buddhists down below.

Saicho had early built his hut in the snows and forests of Mt. Hiei and in the silence and the cold observed his austerities. Said to have been but a youth of

eighteen, he had climbed the mountain and sought the way, relying on what he had learned while in Nara.

One day he came across a fallen tree at the very summit of the mountain. From it he carved an image of the Yakushi Nyorai, that manifestation known as the Buddha of Healing (Bhaisajyaguru Tathagata). This figure—788 is the date given—he then set up in his hut. The house became home to the image and turned into a temple.

This was beginning of Enryaku-ji, and the little dwelling itself was eventually to be transformed into the mighty Komponchu-do where, it is said, this same image still stands outlined in the shadows by the "inextinguishable Dharma Light" that Saicho himself lit and which, says the temple, has been burning for over twelve hundred years.

卍

It was in 804, after this impressive beginning, that Saicho traveled to China, returned with the precepts of what became the Tendai sect in Japan, and consolidated his mountain temple.

Tendai was broadly Mahayana and its basic scripture was the so-called Lotus Sutra. This purportedly contains the Buddha's final sermon, in which he revealed the potential buddhability of everyone. At the same time, it bolstered this with ecclesiastical authority, and was itself much concerned with doctrine, attempting a grand synthesis of all religious knowledge.

By 823 the place was so powerful that the emperor Saga was prevailed upon to confer it with the name of Enryaku-ji—after the year of its founding—and to announce its official role of protecting the new capital and his imperial highness from the malevolent forces of evil inhabiting the northeast.

Beside protecting the city, the purpose was also to promote this new Buddhism which would combat the narrow Hinayana influence of the Nara temples. Saicho called his monastery Ichiji Shikan-in, a name which refers to the possibility of attaining Buddhahood inherent in everyone, one of the tenets of Tendai. This was in pronounced contradistinction to Nara Buddhism which insisted upon the concept of Sanji, interpreted as the inherent inequality of people and the consequent acceptance of a hierarchical society.

It was here, in the nearby Kaidan-in, a smallish red-lacquered building, that a year earlier in 822 Mahayana Buddhism (to which Tenryu belonged) officially declared its independence from the Hinayana Buddhism of Nara. The ecclesiastical threat had passed—the new Buddhism was benevolent.

Its duties also included prosylatization. Saicho, on his deathbed, ordered his disciples: "Do not make images nor copy sutras for me. Rather transmit what I have taught you. Spread my teachings so they will be useful to all."

Enryaku-ji had other roles to play as well—these largely political. As this liturgical capital grew ever larger it began to exercise an influence upon the imperial government and consequently upon the country at large. This was apparently one of Saicho's intentions.

In a manual for Tendai monks (the *Tendai Hokkeshu Nembun Gakusei Shiki*) he wrote that students should strive to become *kokushi* (national teachers) for "as students of the teachings of our Enryaku-ji Tendai lineage, even if we are beggars on the street, we can still become the emperor's teacher." As a *kokushi,* one was to travel throughout the provinces and instruct both officials and citizens. In this way religion, in particular the Tendai religion, could became the basis of the Japanese state. "Repay your indebtedness to the country by spreading the word" was the slogan oft repeated.

卍

Enryaku-ji was quite strong enough to enforce these teachings. Eventually it extended twenty miles east and west, and twenty miles north and south, occupied the entire top of this large mountain and had a circumference of two hundred forty-four miles. In this enormous area there were more than three thousand buildings and it was said that the number of the priests and monks and servants was uncountable.

Its position was in several senses unassailable, a fact voiced by a later poet, Ji'en, who wrote:

> Many are the mountains
> But when we say 'mountain'
> We mean Mount Hiei.

On different levels, there are seemingly endless staircases, and vast distances between the various parts of the compound. In addition the training was so rigorous that those who did not leave or die became exceptionally strong.

And it is always cold. Mount Hiei is over two thousand five hundred feet high, not really great as mountains go, but quite lofty enough to ensure snow through three seasons. There are also frequent winds. Those who lived and studied on Mount Hiei had to be strong soldiers for Buddha.

The main political tool of this enormous ecclesiastical citadel was an army of militant warrior-monks. Originally Buddhism had had no military arm. Nara Buddhism was a strictly aristocratic affair and the court limited those few members who did not belong to the aristocracy. With the move to Kyoto, however, such rules were relaxed and the large outlying temples began hiring an increasing number of peasants who were to serve as private armies—initially for protection, later for aggression and gain.

These warriors were called *akuso* (rowdy monks) and so they were. Whatever northeast evils the emperor Kammu had wished to avoid, they could not have been more troublesome than the monks themselves.

From 969 on the cenabitic army frequently threatened the court with violence, and in later years often carried out these threats. Imperial concern was voiced by the later emperor who is supposed to have said: "There are three things I cannot control—the Kamo River, gambling, and the monks on the mountain."

Since police were forbidden in the sacred precincts of Mount Hiei, Enryaku-ji itself became a refuge for those on the run from the capital. Professing religious enthusiasm they clambered up in such numbers that finally the head bishop Kakujin (1012–81) announced that the monastery would form its own army to rid "the temples and the estates of thieves and robbers." This army, however, was comprised of these very thieves and robbers. Enryaku-ji had, ironically, itself become the dreaded northeast threat.

The real enemies of this ecclesiastical military were not the court's aristocrats but other sects, their rivals for power. Originally the non-Nara sects, Tendai and Shingon, had been weak enough to coexist. But no longer. By the tenth century the conflict between the *sanmon,* or "mountain faction" based at Enryaku-ji, and the *jimon,* or "temple faction" based at Mii-dera, led to armed struggles which lasted from 933 to 1571.

The Tale of the Heike, that medieval war chronicle, has many passages concerning the militant monks, the power they enjoyed, and the damage they inflicted. They often intimidated the emperor and in 1177 burned the imperial palace causing a conflagration which destroyed much of the capital.

"Fanned by a strong southeast wind" says *The Tale of the Heike* "flames like huge cartwheels leaped three and five blocks and burned diagonally toward the northwest in an indescribably terrifying manner. . . . Family diaries, documents preserved for generations, and treasures of every description were reduced to ashes. The losses may be imagined. Hundreds of people perished in the flames, as well as countless oxen and horses. [But] that fire was no ordinary occurrence. Someone had a dream in which two or three thousand big monkeys, each carrying a lighted pine torch, came down from Mount Hiei to burn the city."

From the eleventh to the fifteen centuries the Enryaku-ji army was the most powerful in the country. During the thirteenth century alone it descended upon the capital more than twenty times; it controlled all the religious and political affairs it could, and, like any political organization, was ruthless in suppressing its rivals.

All new religious sects had to contend with the Tendai monks of Enryaku-ji. Even though most of the leaders of these newer beliefs had been trained at the temple, no ties bound the graduates. The mountain monks continued to raid the new temples, burning their records and killing their priests. When Nichiren (1222–82) attempted a beginning in the capital, the holy Tendai army razed all twenty-one of his temples, and butchered all of his monks—in a single temple three thousand at once. Even today the Nichiren sect, strong in the rest of Japan, is not a major force in the old capital.

Enryaku-ji's reign as a center of military power continued into the sixteenth century. Then, in 1571, "hardened by age, blinded by success," as one chronicle describes it, Enryaku-ji sided against Oda Nobunaga, the general who succeeded in ending more than a century of civil war and eventually was to bring the entire country under his control.

Oda is supposed to have looked up at the militant monks and said: "If I do not take them away now, this great trouble will be everlasting. Moreover, these priests violate their vows: they eat fish and stinking vegetables, keep concubines, and never unroll the sacred books. How can they be vigilant against evil, or maintain the right? Surround their dens and burn them, and suffer none of them to live."

Though the priests were supported by a number of the powerful, including the shogun Ashikaga Yoshiaki, they could not prevent the army of Nobunaga from storming the mountain, burning the temples, and slaughtering some three thousand priests. On the twelfth day of the ninth month of the year Genki (September 30, 1571), all the buildings, all the records, all the treasures of eight centuries were destroyed. Of the greatest temple complex in Asia not one building remained.

The heights of Mount Hiei, like much of the capital, remained deserted until after Oda was assassinated in 1582. His successor Toyotomi Hideyoshi then began a program of reconstruction. Since he himself had imperial ambitions, he rebuilt Kyoto on the model of the imperial capital it had once been. He even recalled the example of the emperor Kammu, who originally allowed no temples in the city itself, and placed the hostile Jodo and Nichiren temples where they could be watched—creating Teramachi in the east and Teranouchi in the northwest. He allowed the Tendai sect to reopen its notorious complex at Enryaku-ji but limited it to one hundred twenty-five temples. It never again wielded secular power.

卍

In the Komponchu-do, rebuilt in 1642, the Yakushi Nyorai is said still to stand and so it may—it is impossible to tell in the darkness. Across bare, cold, red-lacquered floors now long rubbed pink, the barefoot visitor slides into the shadows of the great central hall and there, between the further pillars, opens a gulf.

Ten feet below, faintly illuminated by candles stands the personage. Seen as though across the moat of darkness, it is perhaps the statue carved by Shicho many centuries ago. Near it is that perpetual lamp said lit by the founding monk. Though it was in fact put out by Nobunaga when he began his depredations, this fact is ignored and it burns as though it has always. Yet it reveals nothing—the figure before it remains in the darkness.

The muffling scent of incense hangs in cold air and there remains something of the militant blackness of the huge, brooding, vanished complex. The heavy roofs weigh in the cold mountain air, the great cryptomeria stand black over the still temples, and still flags hang from the high eaves—yellow, green, red—speaking of old China and beyond, to ancient, cold Tibet.

In the dark of a winter afternoon the great icy Komponchu-do seems—as do all frozen things—to be waiting. The single lamp, cold as the gulf in which it burns suspended, is the only sign of life—the sign of a life to come.

Enryaku-ji • **35**

Ishiyama-dera

石
山
寺

The old Japanese guidebooks to the temples of Kyoto make much of the masculine nature of Enryaku-ji. There were many reasons for doing so but among them may have been a desire to celebrate the perceived femininity of Ishiyama-dera.

This temple is not on the stern heights but rather on a gentle eminence along the Seta River above Lake Biwa. Open, easy of access and pleasant of aspect, Ishiyama-dera also has a long history of women visitors.

The author of the *Kagero Nikki,* known to history only as "the mother of Fujiwara no Michitsuna," took refuge here during troubled times. The Lady Murasaki is said to have penned part of *The Tale of Genji* while staying here.

The date of this occurrence is known (the night of the full moon, August, 1004), the room is identified (right off the *hondo*), and in a way she is still there. In her many-layered robes (the outer one purple—*murasaki*), brush in hand, a blank page on the desk, sits a mannequin with long hair and whitened face purporting to be the famous author.

She has just paused in her inspiration and is looking at us—peering into the future. She seems to be pondering a narrative problem—it appears to be a grave moment. Indeed, it may be because, according to the Noh drama *Genji Kuyo,* the Lady Murasaki was actually an incarnation of the local deity, the Ishiyama Kannon. She had written her novel solely, you see, in order to teach the Buddhist truth that the world is but a dream.

Later, many other women also came. The hero of Saikaku's *The Life of an Amorous Man* was here enjoying the view over Lake Biwa, and overheard a most attractive lady explaining to a companion that this was the very spot where *The Tale of Genji* was composed. Intrigued, he drew closer and, in so

doing, caught the lady's sleeve on his sword guard. Or she caught his. In either
event they became lovers.

Others to take advantage of the place included a number of women who
over the centuries found in Ishiyama-dera a place of refuge. These remain
unchronicled but their number is suggested by the popularity of the "con-
cealed Buddha." It was here that women came to pray for easy childbirth, for
a good marriage, and for deliverance from a marriage which had turned out
bad. A presumed gift of the famous Prince Shotoku, this "invisible" Buddha
gave hope to many generations of women and is, in fact, still much visited.

All of this has given the place its feminine aura. Consequently the interiors
of the temple rooms have been found domestic in appearance, redolent of
kitchens and pantries, of a genial, family-like clutter. I was not surprised to see
one of the priests over in the corner, chopsticks out, eating his lunch.

When Buddhism moved from the plains of Japan to the lower mountains, the earlier nature of a personal rather than civic religion was restored.

Shingon, that form of Buddhism which Kukai brought back from China, is centered upon the cosmic Buddha, Vairocana—Dainichi, in Japanese. All deities—Gautama, the historical Buddha, and such beings as Yakushi and Amida and the rest—are manifestations of this entity.

There is only one way for the suppliant to have converse with the deity and come to understand the oneness of all existence. This is through the "three mysteries" of speech, body, and mind which can be coordinated in rituals that require the worshipper to very much rely upon him or herself.

Among these mysteries it is speech which most important. The oral recitation of spells results in "true words" (*shingon*). All religions have their spoken prayers but Shingon has incantation, mantra recitation, and a rich variety of *shomyo* chant.

This codification (along with the iconography of the *mudra* hand positions and such pictorial devices for meditation as the mandala) much appealed to the early Shingon believers. These came to include practically the entire Heian court, an aristocracy not only delighted by the rituals and ecclesiastical trappings of Shingon but also reassured by its fixed hierarchy, and its pantheon of deities—headed of course by Dainichi.

The religion seemed designed for the aristocratic court—even the main deity suggested this. Dainichi, the name of this transcendent being, is in Japanese written with the characters for "great sun" and so there was the opportunity to identify him with that supreme imperial deity, the Shinto Sun Goddess, Amaterasu Omikami.

Also appealing to a closed aristocratic society was the exclusive, esoteric, and personal character of Shingon. In theory this religion might give lip service to the universality of Mahayana Buddhism, in practice, the rites were complex and so time-consuming that only leisured aristocrats could have had time for them.

An indication of the extraordinary popularity of Shingon in places of power was that Enryaku-ji, the Tendai temple up on the mountain, also evolved its own form of esotericism. This, like the original Shingon itself, was a form of tantrism—that branch of Mahayana Buddhism which traveled particularly well and is still seen (to the extent that Chinese occupiers allow) in Tibet.

Japanese tantrism—Shingon—became, like all of Japan's imports, safely domesticated. While the tantric ceremonies of the Indian Shakti sect spectacularly dealt with death and destruction, with living sacrifices, Japanese tantrism did no such thing. And over the centuries it became more and more refined. Eventually, the esoteric quality of the religion confined itself to the fact that the "secrets" of Shingon are only properly passed from one religious officer to his adept—and not to the general public. It remains personal and, though not without a certain civic aspect, it still turns inward.

卍

Ishiyama-dera was among the first temples to neglect a careful citification, to instead cultivate a certain rustic look. With its rocks (*ishiyama* means "stone mountain"), its many gentle levels, and its modest heights, this temple seemed to be almost an elegant country residence. Too, the rocks themselves (wallastonite, an odd combination of limestone and granite, white, it was said, as a woman's skin) are decorative to a degree. The "mountain name" of the temple is Shakkozan which means "Shining Rock Mountain."

Shine these rock gardens do. Dazzled in the early spring sun, I approached and found that the reason was not solely the stone itself. The surfaces were studded with one-yen coins, left there, perched in the porous holes of the stone, imbedded in this crack or that—all of them reflecting the light. Reflecting also the friendly faith and assured trust of the worshippers—their relaxed confidence in their religion and its domesticated temple. I saw no coins left hopefully behind at Enryaku-ji.

卍

Speaking of money, it was said to be in the year 749 that the emperor Shomu requested the famous monk Roben Sojyo to pray for gold. Though it was unusual for a Buddhist clergyman—even of the Nara persuasion—to so openly concern himself with wealth, the reason sanctified the request. A large amount of gold was urgently needed for the gilding of that enormous image of the Buddha that was being cast at Todai-ji.

Roben complied by going into retreat and invoking the powers. A being duly appeared (in a dream) and told Roben to go and pray at a place sacred to Kannon, the Goddess of Mercy, at Ishiyama.

This he did and shortly afterward a large amount of gold was discovered, though some distance away in Mutsu, the northern part of Honshu. The Buddha was gilded and a temple was consequently constructed and a new image of the Nyoirin Kannon installed at Ishiyama, site of the providential dream. The grateful emperor designated the temple as imperial and by 754 had presented the library with a set of the Buddhist canons that he himself, it was said, had copied out.

Given the miracle of the gold and the fact of imperial patronage, Ishiyama-dera became popular and before long the image of Kannon was being reputed to possess miraculous powers. Nonetheless, or as a result, it was kept in a special shrine opened to public view only once every thirty-three years.

卍

Yet for all its apparent domesticity and perceived femininity, Ishiyama-dera is still stern Shingon, and it speaks a darker tongue which hints at mysteries that the planned openness of the temples on the plains had largely neglected and for which its own pleasant appearance does not prepare.

It is this aspect of the temple that Ishikawa Jozan (1583–1672), the man who built the Shisen-do, wrote of. With the same romantic hyperbole he was to show in his own structure, he spoke of the towering stones and twisting paths of Ishiyama-dera as a true home for the immortals; its fantastic rocks and cave-pocked cliffs as fit hiding places for spirits. Basho was also here and noticed this the dark quality when he wrote that cooler than the white rock was the autumn wind.

Ishiyama-dera most reveals this nature when the spring sun sinks, the twilight gathers, and the temple begins to look more like how we think a far mountain temple ought to appear.

Tanizaki Jun'ichiro, the famous novelist, has elucidated upon this. The heavily tiled roofs cast deep, spacious shadows. These "so dilute the light that no matter what the season, on fair days or cloudy, morning, midday, or evening, the pale white glow scarcely varies. . . . This was the genius of our ancestors, that by cutting off the light . . . they imparted to the world of shadows that formed there a quality of mystery and depth superior to that of any wall painting or ornament."

In contradistinction, Chinese-style temple compounds such as some in Nara with their regular structures, seem full of light, illuminated as it were by their very openness. Theirs was a place of assembly, a social area, which served well the collective need.

But Buddhism as a religion also had need of its places of refuge, areas of retreat. Prayer is essentially private—this is something which Shingon knows. The altar is black until the candles are lit. The most important ceremonies are early in the morning, in the last dark before the sun rises. The worshipper kneels alone and contemplates both darkness and self.

Temples cultivate shadows. Very few Japanese things traditional were made to be seen in the bright light which now illuminates them. Electrified Kabuki looks flimsy and garish because it was meant to be viewed only by massed candlelight; black lacquer seems mottled and dull because it was made to be seen in dimness, its surface reflecting only ambient light. The Great Buddha at

Todai-ji in Nara with its giant lotuses and attendant bodhisattva looks like backstage at *Lakmé* because all of this detail was never meant to be so plainly viewed. Turn off the lights and the statue again assumes its dim presence. This can be comforting. The Yakushi Nyorai waits in the medieval cold, the invisible Kannon remains in her chamber.

Yoshida Kenko (1283–1350), a retired court officer, would later write in his *Tsurezuregusa,* known as *Essays in Idleness,* that visits to temples are best made by night. Very true—and here in the civilized shadows of Ishiyama-dera one again remembers that darkness is a friend to religion.

卍

Such might have been the sentiments of the emperor Go-Shirakawa (1125–92) who, troubled by the wars which so marked his reign, made a pilgrimage to Ishiyama-dera and there, on the gentle heights sat in the elegant Tsukimi-tei, the moon-viewing platform (still there), and soothed himself by watching the full moon rise over the distant hills.

Behind him waited the future. For dwarfing his moon-viewing platform, in but a decade or two, was to stand the Tahoto, built by Yoritomo, the Kamakura shogun, one of the undeclared enemies whom Go-Shirakawa was now escaping by coming to meditate.

This large structure is called a treasure tower (and is in fact now a National Treasure—and the oldest, as well as the most beautiful, of all such extant towers: it used to be on the four-yen stamp, back when four yen bought anything) and is quite indicative of the "development" that went on when the Kamakura shoguns took over.

However, at that time, Go-Shirakawa had the place all to himself. Sitting there, facing the great silver orb, he gazed below at the river shining in the reflected light. Were he there now he would see mainly the new *danchi* apartment complexes—a modern form of development—which so disfigure the shores of the river, but back then it was just emperor, moon, and darkness.

It would be too much to suggest that the emperor Go-Shirakawa was actually praying, but he was probably enjoying that state of inner peace which stillness and the dark and the inward gaze can bring. And this is in itself a kind of meditation, an inner communion very near prayer.

Kiyomizu-dera

Once much larger, Kiyomizu-dera now consists of a modest seven halls, a three-story pagoda, and several minor buildings. The main hall, however, remains anything but modest—it is one of the most spectacular structures in all Kyoto—and it opens onto an enormous verandah built out over a cliff which offers a spacious view of what is left of the skyline, and itself presents the most distinct ecclesiastical profile in the capital.

The temple, given its spectacular presence, its lofty bastions, and its general eminence, was early known as the "Mountain" and a recent abbot, Ryokei Onishi (1876–1983) was still saying, at the age of 107, "When you climb this Mountain, you are approaching the Buddha. And if you come every day, you draw even nearer."

Kyomizu-dera was originally intended, with its many pillars, its open space, and its splendid view, to represent Kannon's southern paradise—or did before the view was ruined by the cheap impertinence of Kyoto Tower, as distinguished from the expensive impertinence of, say, the nearby Nijo Castle.

Like Amida's western paradise, represented in the Byodo-in and elsewhere, this paradise of Kannon was an idealization of the world to come. A land of flowering trees, cooling waters, this idea of a future paradise came perhaps from some dim memory of the royal pleasure gardens of the Near East which had earlier inspired the garden complexes of the Tang Palace. Certainly, the artificial paradises of Japan followed this Chinese scheme and in these versions the imperial park came to mirror on earth the beauty of a celestial future.

Kiyomizu-dera suggests that paradisical ideal though a oneness with the landscape it occupies. The great cypress-shingled roofs are continuations of

the cryptomeria-covered hills and the verandah is a huge cave in the side of this manmade mountain. If Amida's paradise is a celestial palace, Kannon's here is a heavenly hall animated by nature itself. If a visit to any temple is often like a stroll through a grove—all of these wooden pillars, the leafy overhead of panels and paintings—it is here a journey through an entire ecclesiastical forest.

Below this pillared esplanade is the Otowa no Taki, the Sound-of-Feathers Waterfall and believers like to refer to it as the original source of the *kiyomizu* (pure water), its presumed soundlessness being but one of its miraculous qualities. It is to be drunk from long-handled cups, and those who stand under its icy stream become even more purified.

From here the path leads up a small hill to tiny Taiza-ji. While the temple is undistinguished, the view is unsurpassed. Here, across the small valley, rears the entire complex of Kiyomizu-dera. It is like a city, saddled across the ridge, roof after roof, the view commanded by the great hall and its enormous esplanade, the visitors now mere dots of color in the vastness.

Architect Ashihara Yoshinobu has noted that Japanese architecture is only rarely to be viewed from afar, that the mass outline so important to the effect of Western architecture is not often present in traditional Japanese buildings. Architecture viewed from far off emphasizes the whole exterior, that to be seen from closer emphasizes texture and detail.

He also emphasizes the difference between exterior (outside) and interior (inside). The latter he feels is the more Japanese, for in the matter of form and content the Japanese are interested in content (the inside) and the classical West in form (the outside). This is true and Kiyomizu-dera is the exception that proves it.

But observing form, architecturally or otherwise, is also a way of seeing universality, a manner of regarding essence, the timeless, the invariable. It leads to introspection.

"The only sightseers left on the verandah of the temple were a few girl students, but their faces were not clearly visible. This was the hour Chieko had come to prefer. Votive candles were burning in the dark recesses . . . the verandah was built overhanging a cliff. Like the light, buoyant bark roof, the verandah, too, appeared to be delicately suspended . . . Chieko leaned against the railing and gazed toward the West. She spoke abruptly: 'Shin'ichi, I was an abandoned child, a foundling.'"

Thus the heroine of Yasunari Kawabata's 1962 *The Old Capital* finds in Kiyomizu-dera the strength to tell her secret. And in the penultimate sequence of Ozu's 1949 *Late Spring,* father and daughter make their last trip together to Kyoto and stand on the great porch, differences forgotten, lost in the peace of perfect space.

卍

Legend says that long ago the wandering ascetic monk Enchin one day arrived in the hills of Higashiyama, to the west of the plain on which the capital was to rise. There he met a devout follower of the goddess Kannon named Gyoei, who had a dwelling next to a small waterfall. Invited in, the monk stayed and made himself useful.

Kannon was, of course, already there. The Buddhist hierarchy begins with the Buddha himself in all of his various aspects—Amida, et al., then these manifestations are subdivided as we have seen into *bosatsu* (bodhisattva), compassionate beings who postpone their own nirvana in order to save those still living. Since they are the ones who do all the work they are commonly portrayed as standing or even flying. As attendant to the Buddha, Kannon herself was an early visitor to Japan—she was already at Ishiyama-dera. A bodhisattva, she attends the Buddha in his Amida manifestation.

Kannon is thus seen as the personification of infinite compassion. Indeed, her name so indicates this quality: Kannon—Guan'yin in Chinese—is taken to mean "the one who hears all cries." Originally male in India and known as Avalokitesvara, Kannon's gender changed at some time during her long history. Being a man, however, was just one of her incarnations. The Lotus Sutra says that she has thirty-three of them. Still, the female form has been perceived as most fitting.

Also, Kannon is attendant to the Amida and can thus provide protection during the present life and help in transporting the faithful to Amida's Pure Land after death. She was from early on an important and popular deity.

Much of this information was doubtless included in a sermon which Gyoei delivered to a passing officer, Sakanoue no Tamuramaro. This military man went on up the mountain after that and successfully accomplished his mission of capturing some local bandits. Sakanoue came to the conclusion that this success was resultant of the sermon—or at least this is the decision that he comes to in the Noh drama *Tamura*.

In any event grateful, he had a small temple built for Gyoei and Enchin which they named after the waterfall, the Temple of Clear Water, Kiyomizu-dera. This event is now dated as having occurred in 788—some six years before Kyoto itself was founded.

Soon afterward, a newly made image of Kannon (impressive and all inclusive—it is said to have had eleven faces, a thousand arms, and a thousand eyes) was in place and the temple was in business. But Gyoei had mysteriously

vanished. It was then that Enchin discovered that the now absent priest had really been a manifestation of the androgynous Kannon herself. This led to a suitable number of pilgrims, and by 804 the emperor Kammu had made this special temple a large grant of land.

He also, having moved to the new capital, gave the monk Enchin and his military patron the old imperial *shishin-den*. This enormous throne room was moved to the sacred precincts where it served as the main hall. As Bruno Taut noted, temples are really homes (and a throne room is part of a home), somewhere to put the deity. And it was here that Kannon made herself so comfortable that when private ownership of temples was prohibited in 810— a late attempt to stem priestly influence—Kiyomizu-dera was already an important religious center.

The religion was Hosso, that sect of Amiditic Buddhism devoted to the worship of Kannon. The name comes from the character for *dharma*. This quality cannot be explained but, as one early priest put it, "We cannot see air, but when it becomes cold, rain turns to snow: this is *dharma*. Basic laws (*ho*) are thus given form (*so*)."

The few remaining Hosso temples were Horyu-ji, Yakushi-ji, and Kofuku-ji—all in Nara. Kiyomizu-dera enjoyed brotherly (or sisterly) relations with most of them and thus had to endure the jealous enmity of that almost equally old but much more quarrelsome monastery further up on the mountain, Enryaku-ji .

These military monks often descended and destroyed Kiyomizu-dera. In *The Tale of the Heike,* there is a full account of one such attack that tells how they bore down on the place, burned every last one of its halls and cells to the ground, and butchered whomever they could find.

Yet, despite being many times destroyed, the main hall has always been rebuilt, more or less in this early palace style (that which we now visit is a seventeenth-century copy) and Kiyomizu-dera maintained its eminence (it is high on the list of places sacred to Kannon and thus a place of lucrative pilgrimage) and it continues to prosper.

卍

Kiyomizu-dera retains something of the reverence which the architecture demands and which Kannon herself requests. Long ago, Sei Shonagan on one of her outings about the capital decided to make a retreat to Kiyomizu-dera. She had often been there and apparently liked it. She had indeed already written of listening there with deep emotion to the cries of the cicadas, but now it was autumn and so she wrote: "Going to Kiyomizu, I was about to start climbing up to the temple when I noticed the smell of burning firewood. I was so deeply moved by its charm."

Mii-dera

Until well into the Tokugawa period (1600–1867), Japanese political history was all but inseparable from a chronicle of religious wars—Japanese history was Buddhist history. Among the temples most often affected by these constant political battles was Mii-dera. One chronicle dated 1319 says that it had already been burned to the ground as many as ten times.

Located below Mount Hiei along the shores of Lake Biwa, this temple was originally known as Onjo-ji. Founded in 774 by Prince Otomo no Yota, it was the headquarters of the Jimon branch of the Tendai sect. Its popular name of Mii-dera originated in its three wells which were said to have provided imperial bathwater to such seventh-century emperors as Tenji and Temmu. It perhaps consequently had become central to several of the tripartite rituals of Jimon Tendai.

Although this temple began as a branch of Enryaku-ji, the head temple of the Tendai sect, the two establishments soon had a falling out. By 858 the priest Enchin became its abbot and though he had studied under the best teachers in the Mount Hiei temple itself, there was soon a degree of doctrinal dissent.

This escalated into a war between the main Tendai temple and its branch down the mountain. The followers of Enchin were expelled and Mii-dera itself was savaged. Later, Mii-dera was also caught up in the machinations between the imperial house and the newly powerful families of the twelfth-century. Prince Michihito, conspiring against the prevailing Taira, took refuge at Mii-dera, an event which led to its further destruction.

It was in the spring of 1180 that the Taira "sent a force of more than ten

thousand mounted men . . . the monks awaited them at the temple behind moats and barricades of shields and branches. . . . The ensuing battle continued until nightfall, claiming the lives of more than three hundred soldier-monks and their defenders. Then a night engagement began, during which the court's warriors [the Taira] put the temple to the torch after forcing their way inside in the darkness."

The *Heike Monogatari* then continues with a long list of what was lost, concluding that "a total of six hundred thirty-seven buildings and pagodas were all transformed into smoke in an instant, as were one thousand eight hundred fifty-three commoners' houses in Otsu, more than seven thousand scrolls of the Buddhist canon . . . and more than two thousand images."

"Now the auspicious, august place had diminished into nothingness. The exoteric and esoteric teachings had been destroyed instantly; the temple buildings had disappeared without a trace. Naught remained in the precincts where the rituals of the three mystic things had been practiced; no longer did the handbells ring. No summer-retreat flowers were offered; no sound was heard of holy water being drawn from the well."

Yet each time that Mii-dera was destroyed, it was also restored. The phoenix, that heraldic bird, has a place in later temple decorations here for it also has the ability to transform itself from its own ashes and to spring once more to life.

One result is that Mii-dera is one of the four largest temples in Japan—the others are Enryaku-ji, Todai-ji, and Kofuku-ji—and it continues to stretch at length over an enormous parklike expanse above the shores of Lake Biwa in present-day Otsu.

Like Enryaku-ji, it is a city of temples rather a single complex. The *kondo* lies some distance from Kannon-do and involves a long walk and a real climb. There is forest in between and in the spring a profusion of blossoms. There is also, at least now, a pleasant air of neglect—so different from a policed temple such as the Chion-in.

The *kondo* is open—as indeed are most of the temple structures—and anyone can enter. In the incense-scented warmth of this hall (restored in 1599) one may freely wander around in back of the main altar where many of the temple treasures are laid out.

Among these, though not often on such casual view, is a statue of the Miroku Bosatsu, the bodhisattva of the future. Unlike Kannon and Monju and Fugen and the rest—all of whom are doctrinal in origin—Miroku was originally a real person, a disciple of the historical Buddha, and now said to reside in one of the many heavens available.

He is also waiting for his time to return. This is to occur some six thousand million years after the death of the Buddha himself and so there is still an amount of time to be spent before he once more descends to earth and saves mankind.

Until this happens the Miroku Bosatsu symbolizes not only hope but also the precarious nature of life itself. Indeed, with life a series of disasters, religion itself rending its own body, temple against temple, it is scarcely surprising that evanescence became a quality at first tolerated and then celebrated.

The uncertainty of life became, in a leap of the imagination, a consolation. The Lady Nakatsukasa in her diary (1292) penned a poem about the beauty of the morning dewdrops, quietly pleased that it did not take long for these to evaporate in the new light. That national if seasonal passion for the cherry blossom—the *sakura*— is well known. It still continues and is based upon the very brevity of the event. Particularly to be admired are those few days when the blossoms fall and the petals fill the air, symbolic of that Buddhist sense of impermanence (*mujo*) which so continues to inform the Japan sense of life.

This celebration of the transitory, this approval of transience, grew into an aesthetic philosophy. Yoshida Kenko in his fourteenth century *Essays in Idleness* noted with approval the beauty of evanescence. The scroll was beautiful only after the binding had frayed and the ornaments had fallen from the roller. He voiced the same approval in more formal terms when he wrote: "If man were never to fade away like the dews of Adashino, never to vanish like the smoke over Tobeyama, but lingered forever in the world how, things would lose their power to move. The most precious thing in life is its uncertainty."

Ninna-ji

 Temples have different characters, distinct profiles drawn by history. Some are more private, some more public, some more sacred, and some more secular. Ninna-ji has long been an official temple: pubic, showy, grand, imperial.

Founded in 886 by the emperor Koko, this temple—the Omuro branch of the Shingon sect—was built on old imperial grounds far from the center of the city and quite near the pine forests and cherry groves that marked the suburbs of the capital.

Koko himself used to walk among these rustic scenes, as he states in a poem he composed while residing there. He records that while he was out among the pines picking the young spring greens he saw that snow was lightly falling. This combination of the seasons pleased him and so he wrote a poem about it.

It was also on these grounds of the old imperial palace at Omuro, that a temple was constructed and some two years later was inaugurated by the succeeding emperor Uda. And not a year after that the new emperor had abdicated, shaved his head, and taken up residence in his newly built *kondo*.

It was he who, while still ruling, in the height of summer, overcome perhaps with boredom, suddenly desired to see a nearby mountain under snow. So he commanded that its summit be spread with bolts of white silk. This gave the place its name: Kinugasayama, or silk umbrella-hat mountain. It also gave the emperor a certain reputation for frivolity. And it was perhaps thought a good thing that he abdicated.

Such abdications were even this early by no means uncommon. The imperial predilection for retirement, a political tool in China, took in Japan an

almost invariable form. From the sixth century on there was a succession of rulers who gave up the throne.

The reasons for these abandonments were various. One could hide behind the imperial chair and continue to wield authority while the new ruler, holding only its outward semblance, sat idle until, in turn, he too retired into power. Or, the cloistered emperor could immerse himself in the church, though to abdicate and enter religion did not often mean to lead a holy life— rather it was an escape from the demands of a public career. Again, in many cases, abdication was compulsory.

The custom became habitual and the later shoguns followed this imperial pattern as well. By the thirteenth century, as George Sansom has said, we have the surprising spectacle of a state at the head of which stands a titular emperor whose functions are performed by an abdicated emperor, whose real power is delegated to a military dictator whose power is actually wielded by one of his advisors.

With such imperial patronage—from the time of Emperor Uda until the late nineteenth century, the abbots were all from the imperial line—Ninna-ji rapidly grew powerful. Soon it had more than sixty sub-temples, as well as a famous five-story pagoda and the celebrated groves of *sakura*.

Like many places of imperial patronage, Ninna-ji was always among the sterner of the temples, much concerned with protocol and ceremony. Even now it has an serious air. As one enters the Kuro-shoin, for example, the recorded tape begins earnestly instructing, sparing no detail. Still, here this staid concern at least fits the place. Such taped *setsumei* reach a nadir at Ryoan-ji, where the visitor to the superb rock garden is informed in strident tones that, "This is the famous sand garden of Ryoan-ji, a place noted for its tranquillity and famed for its contemplative quiet."

卍

There are many portraits at Ninna-ji. One looks at those faces as they gaze back from scroll and screen: plump, bottom-heavy faces with mild melon-seed eyes and sometimes the decorative topiary of a mustache or a beard.

The outline is known. It is the Heian beau-ideal, the heavy face which reflects good eating, supported below by a girth found attractive in a culture where weight meant wealth.

But this emperor, that bishop, this shogun—did these men look like this? As in China, portraiture in Japan was so late in developing that even now the formula face is the preferred. And back then portraits were lay figures with labels attached.

There was an official beauty for the male from Heian times on. It was agreed upon and the sum of its details meant respectability. What we might find virile, and even physically beautiful, to them repelled. Sei Shonagan watched with disgust ordinary carpenters eating and the Lady Murasaki turned with aversion from the bodies of naked grooms surprised by a palace fire— unforgettably horrible, without the slightest charm, she found the nude body.

For women, however, the beau-ideal was not so carefully composed. Indeed, it was created through subtraction: what she should not have. Her eyebrows were shaved and replaced higher on a surprised forehead, her teeth were blackened, the mouth a dark hole denoting beauty. From the earliest days she was composed—a blank surface upon which men painted.

Furthermore, the creature was invisible: living in shadows bundled into twelve concealing layers, her essence so negative that the nocturnal lover was often not entirely certain that he had the right person.

卍

Yet, like any temple, Ninna-ji was also a place of Buddhist compassion. Kamo no Chomei (1153–1216) in his celebrated *Hojoki* (Record of the Ten-foot-Square Hut) remembered the ministrations of the priest of Ninna-ji as seen from the gate of his hut just up the hill from the temple. It was a terrible time, the years of Yowa (1181–82), when depredations, fires, droughts, and epidemics conspired to bring great hardships to the people of Kyoto.

"People were now dying of hunger, and each day their plight worsened," wrote Chomei. "They were like fish trapped in shallow water. . . . It reached the point where persons of quality, dressed in their fine hats and leggings, did nothing but go from house to house begging for food. Many were overcome by exhaustion and despair in the midst of their ploddings, sinking to the ground where they were. Beside the walls of buildings and along the roads the bodies of those who had starved to death were beyond count. Since nothing was done to remove them, the stench soon filled the city and the sight of them as they decayed was often too ghastly to look at."

Amid this terrible scene Chomei was pleased to remember the priests of Ninna-ji helping as best they could. In particular, the abbot Ryugyo Hoin, who wrote the Sanskrit letter "A" on the forehead of each corpse he found, hoping in this way to assist the deceased to gain salvation since it symbolized the truth of the universe, the contemplation of which ensured the attainment of Buddahood.

Also, despite their pomp the priests of Ninna-ji could be most engagingly human. In fact we know more of this side of Ninna-ji than we do of any other of the Kyoto temples. This is because at the base of Narabigaoka, the same hill facing the grounds, Yoshida Kenko also later built a small house and retired. He could consequently look across the street, as it were, and gaze at the goings-on in the imperial temple.

What he saw he wrote down, among other musings, in his collection *Essays in Idleness.* Many of these entries lament the passing of the old ways. A criminal being flogged with rods is placed on a torture rack and tied to it and Kenko is scandalized that "no one today knows either the shape of the rack or the manner of attaching the criminal."

Many of the more lively entries, however, record what he saw or heard about at Ninna-ji. A young acolyte, drunk at a party, put a small cauldron over his head and danced about to the delight of all. The party over, he discovered that he could not remove it.

Kenko's account continues, saying that the acolyte presented a most strange appearance as he sat in the doctor's office. The doctor himself was most disturbed by the fact that he could find no similar cases in his medical books. So they decided to just pull the cauldron off. This accomplished, only holes were left where the patient's ears and nose had been.

The scene of such painful revels is now long gone. Ninna-ji was—like so much else—burned to the ground during the Onin Wars (1467–77). Unlike many other temples it was not rebuilt until much later. The shogun Iemitsu sponsored its restoration in 1634. Desiring to curry imperial favor he also rebuilt the Gosho Imperial Palace and two of its left-over structures were taken to Ninna-ji and rebuilt as the main hall and the founder's hall. The five-story pagoda and the well-known Nio gate were constructed anew.

In the niches of such gates in the grander temples are found the two Nio guardians. These figures (Benevolent Kings is a translation of their name) display considerable power and serve as ferocious-looking doormen.

Both are quite muscular and stand there half naked. Their names are Bon-ten and Taishaku-ten, originally Brahma and Indra. The mouth of one is open and he is pronouncing the Sanskrit "A" while the other has his lips closed as he is pronouncing the "Un" sound. These are the alpha and omega of Buddhist teachings and symbolize the all-inclusive. Ecclesiastical bouncers.

卍

Ninna-ji remained powerful even though the place was yet again burned down in 1887. Only two tea-ceremony houses were spared. The rest were yet once more reconstructed, this time in the late Momoyama style, which is what we see today. But the imperial prerogative prevails. During the dark days of early winter in 1945, Viscount Fumimaro Konoe went there to worship and, anticipating defeat, wrote the calligraphic plaque which compared the long imperial history to the true light of Buddhism—continuing to shine since the time of the emperor Uda. At the same time, it is said that Konoe went there to meet the emperor Hirohito. Whether there was a plan to retire the emperor is not known. When the Pacific War was concluded in August of that year Hirohito was still on the throne.

Daikaku-ji

The emperor Saga (786–842), son of Kammu who founded Kyoto in 794, made himself a detached palace, the Saga-so, in the far western reaches of the city. There he entertained the local literati, arranged to be posthumously included among the Three Learned Emperors, and led a pleasant life.

Its qualities are seen in the advice he offered when he relinquished the throne to Emperor Junna. "Just stroll among these hills, along these rivers, without concern for rank; take your pleasures with brush or with lute, and have no thought of what you will do next."

He might also have mentioned boating, an activity of which he was fond and in which he often engaged on his own Osawa Pond, a small body of water next door to the palace, designed in tidy imitation of Lake Dongting in China.

Here he also invented the art of flower arranging, though this claim is challenged by that of Ninna-ji which has its own *ikebana* history. The emperor is supposed to have docked at one of the little islands and picked some chrysanthemums which he arranged so as to embody the Taoist Great Triad— Heaven, Earth, Man (*Ten, Chi, Jin*). This gave rise to the Saga school of flower arranging, one which still prospers.

The pond and its artistic associations are also otherwise remembered. Centuries later the emperor Go-Toba stood on its narrow shores and composed a poem about standing by this little lake. Though these shores are much changed from what they once were, that autumn moon now shining is just the same.

The pleasures of nostalgia went well with the historical little pond.

卍

The Saga-so underwent its first transformation in 876 when the emperor Seiwa had the place made into a temple in honor of the founder of Shingon Buddhism, Kobo Daishi. This was named Daikaku-ji, the Temple of Great Enlightenment.

Among the reasons for making the palace a temple was that Kyoto was undergoing one of its occasional epidemics. The emperor was persuaded to make a special offering to the Buddha. This consisted of writing the scripture, *Hannya Shingyo,* while simultaneously reciting it. The resultant manuscript was enshrined in the new Shingyo-den, an octagonal store-house on the grounds of the new temple—and there (though the temple is now concrete) it apparently still rests.

Yet, temple though the palace had become, Daikaku-ji was never a place of ecclesiastical learning, nor even a place of worship. As a later historian wrote, it was a temple where the emperor paid his respects to the deities who had blessed the country. By serving as a medium for carrying out the emperor's will Daikaku-ji had become a place from which the emperor's wishes were made known.

The temple thus remains worldly in the most open manner. There are still modern pleasure barges on the pond and nary a smell of incense in the corridors. That the place was to serve as seat for imperial authority is, however, a fact not without its ironies, because this imperial authority was to be eventually challenged, and at Daikaku-ji itself.

卍

During the era now known as the Period of the Northern and Southern Courts (1336–92) there was a serious dispute between the two branches of the imperial line over the proper means of succession.

Rival courts were established. The northern was at the Jimyo-in, following the emperor Go-Fukakusa. The southern was at Daikaku-ji, following the emperor Kameyama. Rivalry grew into warfare and Ashikaga Takauji—of the family which would eventually take over imperial authority—decided that Daikaku-ji would have to be destroyed.

The event is laconically noted in the *Daikaku-ji Fu* (The Chronicles of Daikaku-ji). "There was a fire on August 28, 1338. The temple halls and priests' quarters were completely destroyed. Though they were rebuilt, the new structures never reached even half the size of those previous."

Fifty years later, the glories of Daikaku-ji were still being remembered. Emperor Go-Kameyama wrote with nostalgia of the grandeur of an age now past. His sleeves were wet from wiping his eyes, he said, as he wept over times of peace long gone.

For Go-Kameyama, who ruled from 1383 to 1392, war was always present. The battles of the Onin destroyed much of the capital and it was not until the unification and the Tokugawa period (1600–1867) that the longed for peace was achieved—at great cost.

In 1626 Daikaku-ji was again reconstructed when the emperor Go-Mizunoo donated his imperial hall of state as the new Shinden, which he then had lavishly decorated with many paintings and screens. In front of the reconstructed hall he also had planted (a tradition of the imperial garden plan) a wild orange tree and a plum tree to the right and left of the main entrance.

None of this improvement could, however, quite obliterate the sense of space which still permeates many of these ancient temple compounds. Just as the easy curves of the Ishiyama-dera roofs, the latticed verandahs, and the paneled doors recall even now the grace of Heian times, so, too, the spaces of Daikaku-ji retain still something of those ancient years.

卍

How fittingly emptiness suits places of worship. Perhaps this is because we are to fill it ourselves. Lao-Tzu in the *Tao Te Ching* pointed out that kitchenware is useful only for its hollowness, and houses can be lived in only because they are empty. A temple, just as a church or a mosque, must be filled with space. Like a pot or a pan it defines a void.

At Daikaku-ji, this void is made civil because of its long tradition of imperial ease. The rooms are punctuated by regular *shoji* which let in light and at the same time transform it. The sections of the main hall are marked only by low lacquer fences. These are not walls which cut off, they are barriers which enlarge. The altar itself is a presence, standing like an imperial personage in the middle of this space, defining it, marking it, authorizing it.

Byodo-in

 The land where the famous Temple of Equality, Byodo-in, now stands was originally site of several aristocratic villas. The first, in the ninth century, belonged to Minamoto no Toru and the title was passed on to others of his family. It was here that Ukifune washes up after her suicide attempt in the *Tale of Genji*.

Located some distance from the capital at the summer resort of Uji, home of the firefly and the many poems about them, the land was eventually owned by the Fujiwara family—the title descending upon Michinaga and through him to his son Yorimichi. It was this latter who—according to tradition—turned his villa into a temple in 1052.

In honor of the new resident, Amida himself, an amount of rebuilding was done. Just how much is unsure. The center pavilion in the structure—all that remains—was enlarged. But then apparently so was everything else. The originally revised ecclesiastical villa had thirty-three buildings on its grounds, including seven pagodas.

It was in the Chinese style (very fashionable in the capital), had a number of Buddhist innovations—still much in vogue—and the Hoodo, the phoenix pavilion, was built in the shape of that stylish Chinese bird. The result must have been something to see.

The emperor Go-Reizei himself came to look—an unheard of honor—but then, Go-Reizei was both Yorimichi's son-in-law and his nephew, as well as his ruler.

Regardless of calls to duty and obligation, however, imperial curiosity may have been a reason. Byodo-in is still one of the most beautiful Buddhist

structures standing, and in its original form it must also have been one of the most impressive.

It was an architectural metaphor for all nine levels of the Paradise of Amida itself. Still radiant, it must have been gorgeous. A saying of the period indeed endorsed the ecclesiastical potential of the place: "If you long for Paradise, then pay your respects at the noble temple in Uji."

And there, in the central pavilion (the phoenix-shaped Hoodo) sat Amida, that manifestation of the Buddha who presided over the Western Paradise of the Pure Land—a place you went to if you obeyed the precepts of the sect.

When the worshippers facing the hall (facing fittingly west) came to pay their respects they had to stand on the further side of Aji Pond, thought to duplicate the lotus lake of Amida's Paradise, and thus laid out in the shape of the Sanskrit letter "A," a symbol which separates this world of suffering from that world of the Pure Land. From these shores the pious could view Amida himself—though only when the door was open.

You can still what they saw, paradise itself trembling in the reflected waters before it. There are some differences, however. Now that the religious purpose of most temples and churches has vanished, architectural bodies all over the world are displayed as tourist sites. The Byodo-in has even been turned of an evening into a *son et lumière* spectacle, exuding a light never of its own, a paradisical pile, blazing away.

卍

Amida sat (and still sits) inside the Hall of the Phoenix impressively sculpted by the famous Jocho—the only one of this artist's works remaining in Japan. Not only is the statue nearly ten feet high, but it sits alone. Customarily Amida is flanked by attendant deities, Kannon and Seishi, who accompany him in his meditations, but not in this Amida-do.

It was said that the Fujiwaras wanted Amida all for themselves and thus excluded both of the attendants. The deity could thus devote his entire attention to the spiritual welfare of the family. Amida is thus meditating by himself on his golden lotus throne, and his *mudra* —the position of his hands—indicates that he is already in the highest of his nine paradises. Very good at his job, he exhibits a calm and serenity indicating a desirable absence of desire—his lips are neither open nor closed, and his gaze is averted from the view.

This gaze would—were he looking—have included the little lake just at the base of the structure but not the worshippers gathered on the farther shore. Nevertheless this shore became a place of pilgrimage.

The Lady Nakatsukasa, writing in her diary in 1281, noted that when she saw the Byodo-in she well realized why people said it is possible here to envision the splendors of paradise. Even the colors of the autumn leaves she found different and thought they would make fine souvenirs for those left at home.

Here then, in his own personal paradise, Yorimichi knelt and prayed and would have noted with satisfaction perhaps—like his father before him—that, though Amida avoided the pilgrims across the pond, his gaze was directed downward at his famous and powerful worshipper. His father, Michinaga, had indeed died holding a string tied to this very statue of Amida, so that he could the more conveniently be led to the real Paradise of which this below was simply a faithful copy.

This personalized Amida (no one but the family was allowed to pray there: it was institutionalized but not a public temple) remains. From the time of William the Conqueror until now, Amida has sat and endured—thus illustrating one of the precepts of Buddhism. Yet, with the decline of the Fujiwara family the compound was neglected and eventually deserted.

It was also much visited with war and destruction. In 1180 the great battle of the Uji Bridge spilled over into its confines. Minamoto no Yoshimasa, wounded, took refuge in the Byodo-in itself. His two sons, seeking to protect him, were both killed. One was hit in the face with an arrow, the other killed himself in the fishing pavilion (still standing at one edge of the pond) after having suffered many wounds. His head was cut off and thrown under the verandah. The father asked his lieutenant to behead him as well but not until he had penned a final poem.

The scene is described in the *Heike Monogatari* and the poem goes:

No flower of fortune
Has blessed a life resembling
A long-buried tree—
Yet how bitter is the thought
That all should end like this.

Then "without another word, he thrust the tip of his sword into his belly and fell forward, his vitals pierced. Although we would not expect a verse of a man at such a time, Yorimasa had been an ardent poet since boyhood, and he did not forget his avocation at the end."

Later a great fire carried away most of the buildings, including the last pagoda. The Amida-do, however, was spared and sat there until major reconstruction work was begun in 1680—which resulted in the Byodo-in we now know.

The vision of the Western Paradise still floats above the lotus pond and the two ecclesiastically (and architecturally) useless wings of the immortal bird support it so that the whole structure seems to float. It continues to illustrate, what George Sansom has called a successful compromise, a happy blend of temple and palace.

Inside, the paradise itself is still visible. On his throne under his canopy, golden, tarnished, immensely old, Amida still sits with downcast gaze, surrounded by all fifty-two of his own celestial attendants, the *kuyo-bosatsu,* small bodhisattva attached to the wall behind him. They make merry, plucking and tooling on their musical instruments like cherubim or *putti,* while Amida listens with half an ear and the faithful are ravished—for this celestial music is designed to create a desire for the Pure Land.

Like their deity, the frolicking attendants are all originals—except for one, a recent fabrication standing in for the single of these statues which was lost. But this is all that remains. The outlying buildings, the gold inlay, the decorative paneling are gone—but the true treasure is that anything survived at all.

Amida often performed miracles but this is perhaps the greatest: to still exist, a roof over his head, after nearly a thousand years. And to still create the illusion of calm and beauty and wisdom that is the legacy of the past.

Komyo-ji

光明寺

 Buddhism, like any religion, is a living belief. So long as there is a need for it, and there exists the faith necessary, it sustains, lends itself to various activities—only some of them secular—and can achieve great power. Also, like anything living, it changes shape.

By the ninth century the Tang Dynasty was collapsing and Chinese influence slowly waned. So therefore did the religious influences from the continent. Such foreign ecclesiastical authority had been useful, but now when it ceased the semblance of a native religion could evolve.

One of these naturalized products was the Pure Land (Jodo) sect. It evolved from an earlier and originally Chinese Amidism. The bodhisattva Dharmakara (the future Amida) made forty-eight vows which, when accomplished, confirmed his new and more important aspect. Of these the eighteenth became the commonly-called Primal Vow.

This was the promise that Amida would not have become a Buddha unless all those who trust him and invoke his name were to be reborn into his Pure Land, the Western Paradise. Since he *did* become a Buddha this means that the happy fate of his worshipers is ensured.

The concern was for a "good death" (*ojo*), one which guaranteed rebirth in Amida's paradise. This eventually became the aim of popular Buddhism itself. Reforming monks such as Genshin (942–1017) worked to replace the philosophies of the Tendai and Shingon sects with the faith of an instant salvation by Amida, the Buddha of the West.

In his *Ojoyoshu,* a treatise on the "good death," the learned Genshin wrote: "When a pious person dies, Amida appears before him. Kannon brings a lotus flower on which to receive the pious soul, and Seishi stretches forth his hands

to greet him, while all the others sing hymns of praise and welcome. Born into the Pure Land, the pious person is like a blind man suddenly recovering his sight . . . "

Such belief was already fairly common. Both Tendai and Shingon had early, albeit sporadically, encouraged Amida worship. And later Amida developed his own congregation through Amidism as practiced at the Byodo-in and many other places. Among the various statues of East Asian Buddhism on the mainland those of Amida are the most common.

If one questions the advantages of such a demesne, one can only discover need as being the answer. With a good death so important, did that mean that a good life was so impossible? There is no answer but Christians may find a kind of parallel in the way that the "good news" of the personal salvation of Jesus (who also promised a good death), had been greeted. A common paradise is still a paradise whether it be Western or Eastern.

In the newly organized Jodo sect, one which now began a further extension of Buddhism itself, these Amidistic beliefs were incorporated and then, in what we can now recognize as a Japanese manner, both simplified and intensified.

卍

Honen Shonin (1133–1212) the evangelist who popularized the sect wrote that "my method of final salvation . . . is not the sort of meditation such as that practiced by many scholars in China and Japan in the past . . . it is nothing but the mere repetition of the name of the Buddha Amida without a doubt of his mercy, whereby one may be born into the Land of Perfect Bliss."

All that was necessary then was the repetition of the phrase *Namu Amida Butsu*. This was the Sanskrit *namas* (to invoke), followed by the name Amida, and concluded by the title *butsu*. This simplification of Buddhist ideology was not without its critics. Dogen Zenji, founder of the Soto Zen sect, wrote on Pure Land Buddhism in his *Shobogenzo:* "Endlessly repeating the name of the Buddha is like the frogs in the rice field croaking day and night. It means absolutely nothing."

Nevertheless, such simplicity was appealing during troubled times and, said Honen, brought converts "like the clouds in the sky." His success lay in his popular message, but a part of its popularity was occasioned by his own straightforward persona—so unlike the ordinary Buddhist priest of the time.

He had been, according to pious sources, a miraculous child. From the age of nine he was like everyone else up on Mount Hiei in the snowy forests studying the mysteries of the Tendai sect. By the age of manhood, however, he had come to question a religion which offered salvation only to those who had mastered the exceedingly complex nature of its texts.

He read the entire canon of the Buddhist sutras five times over but could find no provisions at all for the manifest tribulations of ordinary people. Then one day, in his forty-third year, he came across a passage in a collection of commentaries on the *Kanmuryojukyo,* written by the Tang priest known in Japan as Zendo Daishi.

"Just repeat, with your whole body, Amida's name. Standing, sitting, walking, and lying down, bothering not about how long or how short the time—just call upon Amida. This is in accord with the Buddha's vow." Upon reading this Honen knew what to do. He would bring the power of the Buddha to the people.

To put it this way is, of course, a base popularization. It is, precisely, to subscribe to the catachronic fallacy—that mistaken notion which says that ideas in one's own time were just like those back then. For example, wondering why feudal Japan just didn't just turn democratic, or why Japan is not more democratic now. The answer is that then, and to an extent now, the idea did not exist.

Bringing Buddhism to the masses or not, however, Honen did exhibit a will to simplify. In addition to his resolve the founder of the Jodo sect was himself a person uncomplicated, direct, and plain. According to Yoshida Kenko in his *Essays in Idleness,* Honen, when asked by an adept how he could say his *nembutsu* when he kept falling asleep, replied, "Recite the *nembutsu* so long as you are awake." Kenko found this "a most inspiring answer."

Others agreed. Among these was the rough-warrior-turned-pious-priest Kumagai no Jiro Naozane. It was he who, according to one legend, helped found the Komyo-in. A disciple of Honen he entered the faith, it is said, in remorse for having killed the young and beautiful Atsumori. This was during the twelfth-century battles between the Taira and the Minamoto clans, at the battle of Ichinotani. This was also the explanation of Kumagai's action given in *The Tale of the Heike* and elaborated upon in a number of Noh plays, the most

famous of which are *Ikuta* and *Atsumori,* and the Bunraku drama *Ichinotani Futabagunki.*

This romantic interpretation is also echoed in a poem written by the aesthete-poet of the Shisen-do, Ishikawa Jozan, who lamented the passing of the beautiful youth, adept with sword and bow, who so eloquently played the flute as well.

"Oh," further lamented the poet, "if he but played a tune on that flute perhaps the enemy would have allowed him to retreat." Or perhaps not.

Actually, Kumagai entered the faith in pique at having lost a law suit involving his ancestral lands back in Musashi. Whatever his motivations, however, he was of value to the church and the moment of his death occasioned the customary miracle of heavenly music, celestial smells, and a large purple cloud on which he rode to the Western Paradise of Amida. This, at any rate, is what the *Honen Shonin Gyojo Ezu,* a thirteenth-century chronicle, says. The more contemporary *Azuma Kagami* says nothing of the sort and gives a more likely death date—1208.

卍

In the Mie-do of Komyo-ji, Kumagai sits in the form of a statue supposedly carved not long after his death. He looks much more the warrior than the saint, and even seems to have a broken nose—either achieved in battle or received through the carelessness of some dusting acolyte—and has his hands fiercely clasped in benediction. He now sits through the ages representative of the enthusiasm for the good death.

His old teacher Honen is also there, along with other clergical worthies. The remains of this saint are said to rest in the Gohobyo, a small building next to the Seishi-do. Though one cannot see it, inside there is said to be a small pagoda which was made by mixing clay with the holy ashes. Other sites, however, also claim the remains so there is no telling.

And in the small garden facing the Hojo, stands the vow of Amida memorialized. Eighteen stones are grouped in threes. Those at front center represent the individual bobbing about in the sea of birth and death, a Buddhist metaphor for this world of ignorance and delusion. The three tall stones represent the triad of Amida himself and his attending bodhisattva.

The person in the ocean need but look up and he will see Amida and realize that he is really in the ocean of the Buddha's great compassion. But this he can do only if he trusts and lets go. Clinging to things—to his thoughts of self, for example—he will see only threatening waves. Once he has abandoned this false self and called upon the sacred name the waters turn smooth as a pond and the radiance of Amida shines forth. This paradox—the sea of wretched karma identical with the sea of divine assurance—lies at the heart of Jodo belief, one in which all questions are answered through faith alone.

Komyo-ji, silent in the western hills, is far away from the railway stations, not on a bus line, and offers its testament in stillness and solitude. The quiet of the maple-lined path leading to the Mide-do does indeed seem to be climbing to a calmer world. And to help you reach this silence is a series of broad stone steps. These dozens of large, heavy, flat stones were brought, one by one, by the faithful for the seven hundredth commemoration of the death of Honen.

Kennin-ji

The priest Eisai, like many others, studied the tenets of Tendai on Mount Hiei. And, like many other ecclesiastics before him, he went to China. There, in 1168 he discovered the discipline of Zen and became convinced that here was something which might protect during this terrible period of *mappo,* the end of Buddhist order. He said so at length in an essay.

According to divine law the history of the world is divided—after the Buddha's entrance into nirvana—into three periods. These are the period of the True Law (*shobo*), that of Imitative Law (*zobo*) and, finally, the period of the Last Law (*mappo*). Throughout these periods the truth of the Buddha and his teachings decline and in this third, though the teachings remain, no one lives by them anymore and hence enlightenment is never attained.

Mappo—estimated to have begun in 1052, just a year before the paradise of the Byodo-in was built—was the background against which such priests as Honen and, later, his disciple Shinran emerged, encouraging believers to depend upon the saving grace of Amida Buddha to lead them from this place of degeneration to the further shores of salvation.

Now, Eisai's claims for Zen began to look equally promising. It was not concerned with the popular good death—if anything it is recipe for a good life, for it seeks to overcome all of those desires which make one so miserable. A product of the new Chinese government we now identify with the Song (Sung) dynasty, Zen speaks of dedication, of inner strength, of the ideal of independence of self. The mercy of Amida is not even mentioned.

This was because, in a sense, Zen predated many of the other sects and was, in fact, nearer original Indian Buddhism than most of the orders that had

already appeared in Japan. The name itself means meditation in the cross-legged position and this is one of the most fundamental practices of Buddhism. The historical Buddha way back at the beginning had meditated in this manner.

Whatever its strong claims as a metaphysical system, however, Zen was also an organized religion and as such could also be put to worldly uses. And no sooner had it reached Japan than these were discovered.

The Hojo regents who had succeeded the house of Minamoto and hence now formed the Kamakura shogunate were indeed looking for just such spiritual relief. Anxious for any indication that change was for the better, and seeking a formula for peace and prosperity, the Hojo regents were busy legitimizing their position by putting up temples and the Zen sect seemed just what was needed.

In Zen there is no canon, no scripture, because words are themselves illusionary, indeed, the aim is for an intellectual vacuum which will allow for enlightenment. Here was also offered a political vacuum through which the Hojos could establish the connection between Zen and the warrior class.

Another reason was that Zen soon became the conduit for cultural imports from China. The Tang Dynasty might be over but the Song offered all sorts of interesting new ideas. Zen itself was one of these and was thus in part responsible for the growth of Song borrowings which had began during the tenth century and grew with Taira overseas trade policies in the twelfth.

Most of the big Zen temples in Japan were soon patronized by warrior families. Not only did Zen search for simplicity, it also encouraged the simple stoicism which the warrior traditionally cultivated. It also sought to transcend the boundaries of both life and death and hence gave the warrior in his dangerous profession a religious foundation for his bravery.

Eisai, back from China, was invited to found a Zen temple. This he did and Kennin-ji was erected in full Chinese style. Indeed, it was patterned after the Baizhang-shan, China's first Zen monastery. Founded in 1202 as the first temple of the Rinzai branch of the Zen sect, it was named by the emperor Tsuchimikado—who gave it the name of the imperial era in which it was built.

The location of the temple—just north of Rokuhara—also suggested that one of its functions was to look after the dead Heike, since Rokuhara was where their headquarters had been. Furthermore, the big black gate which formed the entrance to the new temple was reputed to have been a part of Taira no Shigemori's Rokuhara palace.

The temple's main function, the sole teaching of Zen, was for a time denied it. Both the Tendai and the Shingon sects, having lost their battle against Amidism and the later Jodo sect, now combined to force the new temple to also offer instruction in their faiths. It was not until the time of the eleventh abbot—the Chinese master Lan-hsi Tao-lung—that it became a purely Zen temple.

卍

Besides teaching Zen (it is head of the Kennin-ji branch of Rinzai Zen, third-ranked in the Five Great Zen Temples of Kyoto) the temple also became

known as the place from whence sprang the Japanese cult of tea. Eisai had brought back the plant from China where it was apparently thought of as a medicine. In his *Kissa Yojo-ki* (The Book of Tea and Health), tea was, he says, "a miraculous elixir."

Consequently the court monopolized it. It was connected with Zen, the attractive new religion that seemed to support aristocratic beliefs, or could be made to seem to, and it was good for you, and no one else had it. When it ceased eventually to be drunk solely by the imperials, the clergy got to it and found that it proved helpful in keeping the meditating priest from falling asleep.

On its way to becoming the main ingredient in the famous *chanoyu,* the tea ceremony, its consumption took many forms, one of the most intriguing being a Muromachi period innovation, *rinkan chanoyu,* apparently a combination of bathing and tea drinking. The acceptance of tea was complete when it was discovered to be a remedy for the hangovers of the shogun Sanetomo.

It was the tea ceremony itself, however, that brought new respectability to the beverage. Originally—and even now in its ideal form—this was a gathering of a few like-minded friends, conducted according to an under-stood etiquette in simple and quiet surroundings. The room was small, bare, with only a few beautiful things in it. Tea was drunk and the scroll or the bowl or the flower arrangement was spoken of.

This simple ceremony was, however, soon made substantially more complicated. By the time of the Ashikaga shogun Yoshimasa, it was already an aristocratic and costly pastime; under master-aestheticist Sen no Rikyu it achieved a true elegance in the *chabana,* that combination of tea and the spirit of *wabi*—a much prized sobriety based on an economy of means so stringent that the results (kettle, tea cup) appeared attractively mundane; and in the hands of Toyotomi Hideyoshi, Rikyu's parvenu pupil, it was a Technicolor extravaganza.

The teahouse at Kennin-ji is perfectly traditional: plain, simple, with its classical small entrance through which the guests crawled—the military had to leave behind its swords and social equality was assured. It was built in 1587 by the tea master Toyobo Chosei, and might be seen as sober contradiction to the lavish tea party held during the same year by Hideyoshi at Kitano.

Everyone was invited—literally everyone. From the grandest *daimyo* down to the humblest farmer, all were asked to a ten-day tea ceremony during the course of which were plays and dancing and music and Hideyoshi showed off his tea treasures—rare and expensive tea-caddies, spoons, kettles, the collecting of which had become a fad. One has no idea how everyone from Kyoto and Osaka and Nara and all the towns in between were accommodated. One notes, however, that the farmers had bring with them a cup and a kettle and mat to sit upon, while their betters received no such stipulation at all. One imagines that the monster tea party kept the guests rather well divided; one knows that all this had nothing at all to do with *chanoyu.*

The teahouse at Kennin-ji, though, was about nothing else. Now, however, no one is allowed in, though one may peer through the door. At present it is the abode of a large and elegant but not very friendly cat. Perhaps the animal finds here a place of rest, away from the dogs and tourists. Certainly Kennin-ji itself has a great need for quiet and repose. It is now right off a much run-down Gion and surrounded by bars and pachinko parlors, the grounds themselves filled with the priest's automobiles, the fulfilled desires of this world rank within the holy grounds.

Sennyu-ji

Many temples are on heights. Some, like the Chion-in, require a degree of perseverance to reach. These, like the Parthenon, demand an effort: you are expected to deserve, you earn your exhilaration.

Sennyu-ji, however, is in a valley and from the gate one strolls down the graveled incline to the main hall below. Above is Mount Tsukinowa in the Higashiyama hills, and beyond are the slopes which lead to the Uji River. The pilgrim is in a valley and rolls naturally as ball to stop in front of the great Buddha hall.

The descent into Sennyu-ji seems to fit the secluded nature of the place. It is certainly not a temple like Enryaku-ji which one associates with strenuous heights. Rather, it is a place of quiet contemplation and of rest.

Imperial rest—for emperors are entombed here. Several have left behind a poem or two which reflect the sad history of the later imperial house. The emperor Go-Mizunoo expressed his indignation toward the Kamakura shogunate which so abrogated his authority, comparing the government to those common reeds which impeded the river's natural flow.

Some centuries later the emperor Komei felt the same way about a new set of shoguns, those in Edo (now Tokyo) on the plain of Musashi. Like the useless reeds upon this plain, the rulers up in Edo bowed this way and that, strong but showing how little this strength could be trusted.

Such imperial poetry had, of course, no political influence at all, but the quiet seclusion in which it was written, and by which it was perhaps inspired, remains. Though Sennyu-ji is Shingon, a sect not noted for repose, its attractive air of resignation is one of reasons (along with difficulty of access)

that there are few visitors and none of the hoopla of popular places such as the Chion-in and Hongan-ji to the east and west.

卍

The temple was founded late, in 1218, after the disastrous Minamoto and Taira wars, thus well after the onset of the degenerate age of *mappo* and long after it had been discovered that this world is indeed a vale of tears.

The priest Shunjo (later known as Gachirin Daishi) indicated this in his *Sennyu-ji Kannenso,* a document—now a national treasure—which is still kept in the temple. In it he stresses the need for some kind of spiritual guide in those troubled times. "Life and death are, it seems, the same. The cycle of being and non-being is unending—only devotion can attest to your own realization."

He intended his temple to be a seminary for the study of the tenets of *all* Buddhist sects. Thus spared the direct enmity of Tendai, he was able from the first to ask for imperial aid. His request was granted. The cloistered emperor Go-Toba and his son, reigning-emperor Go-Takakura both donated ten thousand rolls of woven silk which, when sold, raised a considerable amount of money.

Imperial interest insured, it was perhaps natural that the place became the mausoleum for the royal remains, particularly in those later years, when no one wanted them.

卍

One looks at the portraits of the emperors, the full, haughty, blank gazes, all caught in the lineaments of formula, and one senses the common combination of power and pride. The gaze is frontal, from above—one is regarded, but merely that. All of which makes these no different from imperials portraits anywhere.

If one fills in the details, from this chronicle or that history, however, a different caste is lent them. One senses first a kind of fusty, indecisive, bureaucratic motion, a puttering which seems to dither. The singular lack of the pomp of imperial Europe becomes noticeable.

Emperors increasingly wander about their temple-palaces, keep little birds, tend their vegetables, stamp papers, dress up and pose for hours at a time. They play ball in the garden, go boating on the lake, and—of course—stop before they begin. No sooner grown, they are put out to rusticate. Encloistered they write poetry or try to pull strings from behind the arras, or both.

The appearance of an open imperial power is not among those illusions sustained by Japanese history. And consequently, the little hand of the boy emperor seems more human than does the glove of the stuffed kings of England or the manly grasp of the life-sized wax figures of the presidents of the United States.

Also, another reason for this attractive melancholy, is that most of these men lived in the age of *mappo*. To do this was to believe in the grand disaster of the summer sunset and yet to doubt each dawn. It was a time when death and destruction bought submission but promise was held in distrust. This time of easy desperation meant that misfortune was endured or entertained with a resigned satisfaction.

Death brought certainty as birth brought doubt. And history itself became a chronicle of mere misfortune. The arts, like leaves in autumn, turned elegiac, and earlier Tang-flavored Heian times were now viewed as an innocent age of gold when, in the mists of endless summer afternoons, life had been more beautiful because it was further away.

Even the chronicles of Sennyu-ji show some of this longed-for vagueness, this clouded craving for a placid past. The temple believes that it was originally a rustic place founded (as was so much else) by Kobo Daishi, formerly the priest Kukai who brought the Shingon faith from China. At the same time— brought back by the priest Tankai—was what was once billed as the main treasure of the place: a tooth of the Buddha.

Like the relics of the saints, scattered around Europe, the teeth of the Buddha are distributed around Asia. The main temple in Rangoon is supposed to have one and the Temple of the Tooth in Kandy advertises a like possession.

The tooth at Sennyu-ji, however, is now tucked away and none of the literature mentions it. Having heard of its existence, however, I went to the temple office on a cool late summer afternoon and asked where it was.

The priest did not seem embarrassed by this somewhat garish relic—dental records in the halls of the dead imperials—and merely said that it was in the *shariden,* the reliquary. I asked it if were really there and he civilly replied that it was safely immured and so there is no telling whether it is there or not.

Satisfied, I walked slowly up the slope as the sun declined and the cicadas finally stopped. Tooth or none, equally precious, certainly, is the sense of quiet space in these temple yards.

The buildings, with the naturalness of rocks or trees, silently punctuate the air, and I am reminded of Kuko Shuzo's remark that Japanese sculpture and architecture are both characterized by "a taste for simplicity and fluidity [which] arises from nostalgia for the infinite and from the effort to efface differences in space," so that "the distant mountain is often nearer than the trees beside us."

Chion-in

知恩院

 It was here on the grounds of what is now Chion-in that Honen Shonin (1132–1212), who so popularized the Pure Land sect, originally had his dwelling. And it was here that he died at seventy-nine, in what is now the Seishi-do Hall.

When it became apparent that he was not long for this life his followers gathered and desired him to hold a cord attached to the hands of a statue of Amida, a custom said to assist entry into Paradise, and one which even cloistered emperors insisted upon.

Honen, however, refused, saying that he need no such help. He had already noticed Amida and his attendants on their way, and in any event no cord was needed since he plainly saw awaiting him the grand purple cloud upon which he would ride to the Western Paradise.

This occurred but the earthly remains did not long remain untroubled. The always difficult monks on Mount Hiei, jealous at the success of the Jodo sect, took advantage of a series of natural disasters in 1227 to attribute them to the sainted Honen and his teachings. This gave them a reason to burn down his temple. They even wanted to break open his grave located on the hill above the Hondo and throw his bones, like those of a common criminal, into the Kamo River. This plan was thwarted by loyal disciples who removed the master's remains to the suburbs where they cremated them and then, apparently, sent the ashes back to the site of Chion-in.

The temple was rebuilt in 1234 under the sponsorship of the imperial family and by the military, and was thus kept safe from further destruction. In addition, official favors having fallen thick, a whole series of emperors granted Honen ceremonial titles—the last was in 1961 when, upon the occasion of the

750th anniversary of the master's death, the Showa emperor, Hirohito, added yet another.

One of the reasons for the continued imperial interest is that Honen can be seen as an example of filial devotion, something of which paternal rulers have need. But, perhaps even more than to the imperial line this possibility appealed to the shoguns, first the Minamotos from Kamakura, and later the Ashikagas, and then still later the Tokugawas, all of whom desired devoted followers.

Much was made of an anecdote from the early life of Saint Honen. It was said that at a very young age the sage saw his father mortally wounded by bandits. The distraught child at once set out for revenge but the expiring parent in his last breath instructed him rather to stay his hand, to enter a monastery and pray for the afterlife of all. The young saint's filial devotion was apparent.

Such legends are grateful to rulers. As the obedient child to the wise father, so the loyal subject to the benevolent lord. In 1523 Chion-in officially became the head temple of the Jodo (Pure Land) sect (now one of the major Buddhist denominations in Japan), and it remains their headquarters—its subordinate temples, over seven thousand of them, are found everywhere in the archipelago.

The place was richly patronized by the powerful Tokugawa family. Ieyasu himself gave land and built the main hall in memory of his mother. His son built the colossal gate and the scripture hall. After the hall itself was once more destroyed by fire in 1633, it was another member of the family, the third shogun, Iemitsu, who rebuilt it—and it is this building which stands today.

It is somewhat cramped on that imposing hilltop which Chion-in occupies. The two main halls lie at right angles to each other—the Amida-do faces east, the Gaei-do faces south—which disrupts the architectural narrative of the place, particularly after the impressive fanfare of the climb and that gate—the Sanmon.

Chion-in has not only the largest temple gate in Japan—the largest surviving structure of its kind and representative of the massive Zen-style temple gateways erected during the early part of the Edo period—it also has one of the biggest bells in the land. Cast in 1633 it is eight feet tall and nine in diameter. It tolls 108 times at New Year for the absolution of the 108

defilements—an event annually broadcast throughout the nation on both radio and television.

Rudyard Kipling was among those many foreigners who admired the giant bell. "A knuckle rapped lightly on the lip of the bell made the great monster breathe heavily," he wrote, "and the blow of a stick started a hundred shrill-voiced echoes round the darkness of its dome."

Chion-in, as befits a major place of pilgrimage, is now a much developed attraction. Not only is admission charged (a custom common enough in most Kyoto temples) but there is a larger than ordinary souvenir shop and each of the buildings is—like a Disneyland—treated as a special attraction.

There is, in the Mie-do, the very image of Amida Buddha that Honen himself venerated. On the western platform are statues of not only Tokugawa Ieyasu but also his mother and his son. And there are, of course, the Seven Wonders of Chion-in.

These do not include the bell, which is truly wonderful, but rather attractions such as the Uryu-seki, a large rock which is said to have, for some reason, given birth to a cucumber; a sliding panel in the O-hojo, mainly empty, which is said to have once been full of sparrows which were painted in such a lively fashion that most of them flew out of the picture; and the famous Uguisubari no Roka.

These are the floorboards along the corridor leading from the Mie-do to the O-hojo. Under the weight of the walker, these sing like nightingales and, though squeaky floors are common to all temples, they excite much wonder. And some suspicion. The philosopher Umehara Takeshi was taken there as a child and remembers that to him the sound created an ominous feeling.

This was because he realized that the noise was "not for the sake of any artistic refinement, but to prevent the intrusion of scoundrels." He would have not found this odd in Nijo Castle (where the floors squeak as well) because it was a center of political intrigue, "but why would the priests of Chion-in, who had supposedly renounced all worldly concerns, need such a stratagem."

Probably because temples, like castles and churches, are also often centers of political intrigue. This certainly was true of Chion-in, which became a stronghold of the Jodo sect against all others, particularly those which departed from the teachings of Saint Honen.

This legacy was originally in the hands of the priest Shinran (1173–1262), a man who at the age of nine had been instructed by Kannon herself to go to Chion-in and meet Honen. This he did and became a disciple. Before long, however, he found the older priest too conservative. Particularly, he distrusted the emphasis upon priestly celibacy and the endless repetition of the *nembutsu*.

Born just ten years after the beginning of Notre-Dame Cathedral and the establishment of Oxford University, he was a part of a new order which now seems to have occurred everywhere. Playing Saint Paul to Honen's Jesus, he simplified even further the simplicities of Jodo. He said that salvation was possible for those who had never even read any holy scriptures, and the mercy of Amida was particularly available to the unlettered and the immoral. Since "even the good will be born again in paradise," he wrote: "How much more the wicked!"

Here Shinran unknowingly echoes Jesus who said, it will be remembered, that those sinners who repent and pray are more righteous in the eyes of God and more deserving of God's forgiveness than the virtuous Pharisees. Perhaps more Pauline was Shinran's preaching "the glad tidings of salvation," which assure us that through the mediation of Jesus Christ (Amida) the Kingdom of God (the Western Paradise) will become a reality.

Shinran also thought that one need mouth the slogan but once, providing one did it sincerely. "And from that time on, there is no necessity for any other good deed . . . there is no need to fear committing an evil action, for no evil can stand in the way of the original vow of Amida."

He wrote this, not in Chinese, as had been the ecclesiastical habit, but in common Japanese—*kana*—and defended this practice by saying that country people did not know the meaning of *kanji* and were so slow-witted that he had written with the one idea of making his meaning clear to stupid people.

Also, it was perfectly all right for priests to get married—which he did. The bride was said to have been a high-born woman, and though styled a nun, she was still his wife—she bore him six children, all of whom became themselves priests or nuns. So, not only was fertility encouraged but celibacy was frowned upon and the incumbency of Shinran's temples is often still hereditary.

All of this, and much more, has became the basis for the Jodo sect's stepchild, the Jodo Shinshu (True Sect of Jodo). Shinran himself, however, met with disfavor for his revolutionary departures and consequently went elsewhere to find a degree of religious freedom, never returning to Chion-in.

His sect also met competition from the other new religions of the period. Among these was the Hokke or Lotus sect, founded by the priest Nichiren (1222–82). This person attacked not only Jodo Shinshu but all other religions as well. He called the revered Kobo Daishi "the greatest liar in Japan," said that Shingon priests were traitors, that Zen was a doctrine of the devil, and that the *nembutsu* of Jodo and Jodo Shinshu was a hellish practice. When he heard that the enemy Mongol envoys had been executed, he wrote that: "It is a great pity that they should have cut off the heads of innocent Mongols and left unharmed the priests of Jodo, Shingon, and Zen . . . enemies of Japan."

His reasons for such intemperance was that Nichiren believed that *mappo* was the result of the propagation of false Buddhist doctrines. These included any but his own. The Tendai sect had once been based upon his sole authority, the Lotus Sutra, but it had deviated. Desiring to reinstate this original belief, he proclaimed that the Lotus Sutra was the sole authority and that *his* slogan was consequently *Namu Myoho Renge Kyo,* or "All Praise to the Scripture of the Lotus." Having taken the religious name of Lotus of the Sun (Nichiren), thus establishing preeminence, he set about publicizing the new sect.

One of the ways was to set his converts chanting and drumming about the capital, thereby much disturbing the ceremonies in temples belonging to other sects. Another was to opt the entire country. Nichiren was the first to do so and he consequently became the first nationalist. In his tract *Rissho Ankoku Ron* (A Treatise on the Establishment of Righteousness and the Safety of the Country) he wrote, "I will be the pillar of Japan. I will be the eyes of Japan, I will be the great vessel of Japan."

This was a new thing. Never before that a priest so openly sought to counter secular power. And never had a man of the church so equated spiritual welfare with the fortunes of the state. His consequent fall from favor with the Hojo regents meant exile and resulted in there being even now very few Nichiren temples in Kyoto. Nonetheless his militant Buddhism has always proved popular as an off-shoot, as that controversial modern sect, Soka Gakkai, indicates.

Such thoughts seem appropriate at enormous, dusty Chion-in. Though the architecture is quite different from the post-mod designer temples of the new religions, one senses here that popularity is a sign of favor and that when religions become institutionalized, they also become political.

Tofuku-ji

A massive Zen city, its buildings connected by wide avenues, its gorge spanned by the pavilion-like Tsuten-kyo Bridge, over fifty subsidiary temples on the vast grounds, and the whole surmounted by the great Sanmon gate, Tofuku-ji was founded in 1236 by the powerful imperial regent Fujiwara no Michiie (Kujo Michiie) on the site of the remains of Hossho-ji which had been a Fujiwara family temple for over three hundred years.

Michiie desired a temple comparable to the great temple complexes in Nara. In naming Tofuku-ji he expressed this intent by combining one character each from those of Todai-ji and Kofuku-ji, both in Nara.

By this time the ban against temples within Heian-kyo had been long since relaxed and the politicians of the period now perceived that the advantages of an entrenched clergy clearly outweighed the dangers. Religion could ratify and support pretensions to power.

Tofuku-ji was so large and so important that it was made one of the five major Zen temples—the *gozan* (*go-san* meaning "Five Great Mountains," the word "mountain" being homonymous with "temple"). These were Nanzen-ji, Daitoku-ji, Kennin-ji, Tenryu-ji, and Tofuku-ji, all located in Kyoto. Though members were often accused of being excessively pedantic and betraying that spirit of directness which had originally informed true Zen, they nonetheless enjoyed great prosperity. Later famous and powerful patrons included (a cast with whom we are gaining a familiarity) the shoguns of the Ashikaga family, the warlord Hideyoshi, and Ieyasu of the ruling house of Tokugawa.

Its buildings were, however, in the manner of Japanese temples the country over, burned down time after time. Though mainland Asia, like Europe, also presented the melancholy spectacle of a continual destruction, the effect of such constant ruin is particularly poignant in Japan.

One reason is that the archipelago is narrow and the sense of vast holdings, of alternative temple cities saved, is missing. Another is that the nature of Japanese architecture (almost entirely wooden) is of a lightness and—despite occasional grandiose statements to the contrary—of a grace, which makes the fires poignant. It is as though something particularly young or beautiful, of an innocence unprotected, had been destroyed.

In the case of beautiful Tofuku-ji, there was the customary carnage and then, after a major reconstruction in the fifteenth century, the place was left in peace until a great fire occurred in 1881. Only two of the original fifteenth-century buildings survived: the bathhouse (*yokushitsu*) and the lavatory (*tosu*) both of which have been designated Important Cultural Properties.

The latter is the largest structure of its kind. One can look at the interior by gazing through the windows. It was enormous, with regular round holes for the convenience of the users. The contents were regularly ladled out into buckets and then spread as fertilizer over the monks' temple gardens.

Let us pause over this pleasant scene, a Buddhist Brueghel, with hunkered down acolytes and straining deacons. From across the centuries comes this smell of common humanity—one which we note with interest as we watch how human soil returns to its original form in the ground upon which we live and in which we grow while above, in that large and empty late summer sky, a great wheel is turning.

Also surviving is the Sanmon Gate, a national treasure and the oldest Zen-style gate in Japan—runners-up being those at Nanzen-ji and Chion-in. The *san* in the name means "mountain" but is homonymous with the word for "three" and hence to its three stories, to the three gates built into the structure, and to the trinity of sky, air, and earth, which this tripartite structure suggests. There are also elaborate rituals regarding the trinity such as the pilgrim's going thrice through the three doors.

The Sanmon at Tofuku-ji is curious in that its roof is supported at the corners by extra pillars: slim, square supports which were put there at the behest of Hideyoshi. This warlord had heard of a large gate roof somewhere that had just taken off in a high wind, and was determined that it was not going

to happen here in this temple where he had so much invested. To this day these *hashira* are called *Hideyoshi-bashira*.

The *butsuden* and the lecture hall were destroyed in the Meiji fire and were not reconstructed until 1890. But back then a hundred years ago, there were still carpenters who knew how to make temples, and wood so soon weathers that the newness of the structures is not now apparent.

The famous gardens are even newer. Arranged around the Hojo there are four of them and all are the work of Mirei Shigemori who completed them in 1938. The front garden is composed of four rock compositions and symbolized the blessed islands—Eiju, Horai, Koryo, and Hojo. The back garden is composed of moss and azalea shrubs laced in a checkered pattern which imitates the Chinese way of dividing land. In the northern garden the stones are cut square and a like checkered pattern is presented. In the eastern garden, seven cylindrical stones, originally foundation stones from the earlier temple, are arranged in a moss field and represent (for some reason) the stars in the constellation of the Great Bear. There is also the panoramic grand garden with its lake, its islands, its peninsulas. Tofuku-ji thus offers a combination of practically all Japanese garden styles, not just those of Zen.

卍

Originally the garden was right in front of the house and in Heian times thought of as something of an ornamental front yard. Later it adapted itself to other forms, even delineating—as we have seen at Kiyomizu-dera and Byodo-in—an imitated paradise. Under the influence of Zen however, the garden became more of a place for meditation. By the time of the Zen monk Soseki (1275-1321), the garden had become a piece of idealized nature: one which shared little with any presumed paradise, but rather—as in his moss garden at Saiho-ji—created an abstraction which could serve both as focus for meditating spectator and as indication of the temple's importance.

There are three kinds of Zen garden—the *mutai*, garden of nothingness; the *kutei*, garden of the void; and the *sekitei*, or *karesansui*, the stone garden. The abbot's garden at Tofuku-ji is of the latter category—as are the more famous ones at Ryoan-ji and at Daitoku-ji. These "abstract" gardens are often seen as something else. The abbot's stone garden is merely viewed as a representation of the isles of the blessed. That at Ryoan-ji is, depending on the eye of the

viewer, seen variously as a sea with islands, a mother tiger with cubs, a geometrical theorem, or a *koan*.

And there is more. Kenzo Tange has said that "in the stone garden of Ryoan-ji, we feel we are as though shedding our selves . . . but why is it that nonetheless we feel this spirit of resistance? Is it not directed against this spell which draws us from reality and makes us lose our selves? When we go there filled with the concerns of every day no such emotion overcomes us. But it is when we happen to go without thinking, as it were, that this emotion crowds in upon us."

Taoist gardens also indicate symbolic spiritual states, or the psychology of processes. The garden is iconographical: one reads the garden. It is in the shape of an idea—the figurative garden: the pond, for example, seen as *shin* (the character for "heart" or "mind"), or—as at the Byodo-in—the first letter of the Sanskrit alphabet.

Other gardens are, as we have seen, models of paradise. This is true of those in other countries as well. In Islamic countries the garden turns into the rug for greater portability, a paradise to pray upon. In Japan the garden paradise is specifically the Western Paradise of the Amida Buddha, as in Byodo-in, Kinkaku-ji, and many other places.

Another variation and a popular one is the Buddhist garden which includes the famous Buddhist sights. There is a plethora of crane and tortoise islands, each promising good fortune and longevity. There are also countless replicas of Mount Sumeru, the holy mountain which leads to heaven. Like mandalas these gardens illustrate religious precepts.

They do so, however, with the tourist's eye. In the Edo garden there is, as in Edo poetry, a precedent for everything. This pond is really a famous lake in China (named on a modest placard), and that small spit is really Amanohashidate, famous natural wonder from the Japan Sea coast, and that big rock over there is Mount Sumeru—which makes Sumeru the world's first Space Mountain.

Many mandala gardens exist but philosophy is not so favored. Kyoto has a Philosopher's Walk, extending from in back of Nanzen-ji. It is so called because the nineteenth-century Japanese philosopher, Kitaro Nishida, used to walk there. His grandson (quoted by Thomas Rimer) said he remembered going along. "It was thanks to these walks that I was able to visit so many spots famous in the history of Kyoto . . . as we walked along, I would listen to the origins and traditions connected to these spots. And even though I was a child, they affected me deeply, so that I came to know something of history."

Kyoto has, however, no philosophical garden as such. Tokyo does, however—the Tetsugaku-do in Nakano. This early twentieth-century garden approximates the thoughtful life. After leaving the Shisei-do (dedicated to Confucius, Buddha, Socrates, and Kant) you are, as in life, given some choices. If you cross the Bridge of Idealism you find that the A Priori Spring has dried up and so you must search for knowledge elsewhere since mere idealism is not to be trusted. Finally, to reach the summit you must choose between paths—the longer is the Route of Understanding, the shortcut is the Route of Intuition. Midway up the latter route is Deduction Point, a rest place where you can ponder on the way you have chosen. Both, however, end up at the goal, the Station of Consciousness.

Nanzen-ji

One of the most powerful of Zen temples, Nanzen-ji (South Temple of Enlightenment), still presents a picture of what life might once have been like around a large Buddhist center.

For one thing it is, unlike many Zen temples—Mii-dera, for example—still filled with people. Located in the Higashiyama hills, just a short walk from the Heian Shrine, the zoo, and the Miyako Hotel, it is also a part of its own neighborhood: the temple grounds shade imperceptibly to private lots with houses and families.

Another reason for medieval liveliness at Nanzen-ji is that the place is popular enough that the avenue leading to it is lined with restaurants, most of them offering some kind of *kaiseki ryori*—temple food—all of them expensive enough to keep up the tone. If there is the synthetic smell of gentrification there is at the same time the good human odor of things in use. Not for Nanzen-ji that musty scent of old paper, mice droppings, and cat piss which is the standard temple smell.

卍

Like so many Kyoto temples, Nanzen-ji—central seat of the Rinzai branch of the Zen sect—was originally the villa of a retired emperor, a house turned into a place of religion, man retired so that the gods may reign. In 1274 the emperor Kameyama, only twenty-six and very unhappy at the power being usurped by the Kamakura shogunate, decided to step down. He had himself built this restful retreat, complete with two palaces (summer and winter) and extensive gardens.

It was not, however, restful enough: the emperor discovered that he was living not with a deity but with a ghost. When the residence was converted into a temple in 1290 he therefore appointed a priest—Mukan Fumon (Busshin Zenji), from Tofuku-ji—among whose duties was the quelling of the unruly being. This the cleric did through *zazen*. Sitting there deep in meditation, he outwaited the fretful spirit.

Ghost gone, the impressed ex-ruler rewarded the priest by making the appointment permanent and giving him and his sect a portion of the villa land. When the original building, Nanzen-in, was constructed, the grateful former emperor himself carried over a handful of soil to personally place it on the foundation, declaring patronage and encouraging the place to prosper.

It did. Less than a hundred years later, in 1334, Nanzen-ji's importance was such that the emperor Go-Daigo proclaimed the temple first among the Five Temples (Gozan) and hence above all the rest. This included a lot of temples because, though the Gozan originally referred to the "five best," as the virtues of membership became apparent the Five Temples came to include some three hundred.

So Nanzen-ji was important indeed. The impetus was privilege. Abbots and monks were promoted by secular authorities and thus enjoyed benefits denied others. All five were in Kyoto, all were Rinzai Zen and it was this sect of Buddhism that the military rulers had made their own.

The reasons were, as we have seen, various. Chinese precedent (the original pattern for the Gozan came from China) lent probity to a sometimes shaky power structure and Zen Buddhism still carried with it a full cultural complement and an articulated philosophical system. Something like this was desired because both the Hojo and Ashikaga rulers needed a counterweight to the power and influence of the older Buddhist monasteries in Kyoto and Nara which were, in their opinion, too closely connected with the aristocracy.

From this Rinzai Zen system several thousand Soto sect temples were excluded, as well as some Kyoto Rinzai temples such as Daitoku-ji and Myoshin-ji. Its purpose, after all, was to make only *selected* temples all powerful. Thus, though Go-Daigo had originally designated Nanzen-ji as a head Gozan temple, it was the shogun Ashikaga Yoshimitsu who in 1386 elevated it even higher. It was now the leading temple, one of the most powerful, wealthy, and most envied.

Enryaku-ji, jealous as always, sent its warrior-monks down the mountain

and in 1393 burned many of the buildings. But these were at once reconstructed by the shogun Ashikaga Yoshimochi, and later on the temple
commanded the support and protection of not only the imperial court, but
also of Toyotomi Hideyoshi and the Tokugawa shoguns.

At its height Nanzen-ji had extensive grounds in the Higashiyama suburbs
and some sixty-two smaller temples on its property. After the reforms of the
Meiji period, which broke the power of the Gozan organization, however, it
was left with a mere twelve. Nonetheless Nanzen-ji remains among the larger
temple compounds.

卍

The visitor to the South Temple of Enlightenment (Nanzen-ji) now arrives
at the enormous three-story Sanmon, an Edo-period (1626) reconstruction—the "gateless gate" of Zen scripture—though the function is now more
symbolic than actual. You can go through it, but it is no longer in common
use. Two side-avenues carry the cars and trucks and pilgrim-filled buses now
necessary for modern Buddhist life.

It remains the first chapter in the architectural narrative which, like an *emaki*
hand-scroll, is unrolled before the visitor. The gate forms a grand opening
paragraph leading into the passages behind, within the temple compound
proper. Though this form is common to most temples, it is unusually easy to
read at Nanzen-ji. One reason is that an early symmetry has been retained—
the temple is like a mandala spread out on the slopes of Higashiyama.

Many stories are told about the Sanmon. It was, for example, in the upper
reaches of the original gate that the famous thief Ishikawa Goemon was
captured in 1585. He had come to admire the view and in the Kabuki drama
Sanmon Gosan no Kiri (a title which has been translated as "The Fifty-three
Paulownia Trees at the Main Gate") he exclaims at the sight, finding it
particularly beautiful now that the blossoms are out.

Apprehended in the midst of his aesthetic appreciation, he was with his
young son condemned to be boiled in oil in the bed of the nearby Kamo
River. During this, the father held the child over his head before, himself no
longer to endure the torture, purposefully and mercifully dashed his offspring
into the bubbling liquid, then himself collapsed into it. This example of
parental concern is still approvingly spoken of.

Further on, past many another structure, is the Seiryo-den, designated a National Treasure, a building given by the emperor Go-Yozei (1587–1611) from his very own palace compound. Even now it seems more palatial than priestly with its elegant rooms, its covered corridors, and its sense of imperial spaciousness.

Also, despite signs of Buddhist austerity, the style is florid. This is because it is from that period called Momoyama (1568–1600). The translation of the name, Peach Mountain, suggests the style. Though the architecture displays the baroque firmness of the preceding Muromachi period (1336–1573), there is a degree of the ostentatious, an amount of rococo display in the interior decoration.

Just as the Katsura Detached Palace looks back with nostalgia upon an imaginary Heian period, so the Momoyama looks back to an imagined China. In the rooms of the Seiryo-den there is a gorgeous suite, the Tora no Ma, named after the thirty-nine panels by Kano Tan'yu (1602–74) showing tigers (none in Japan and very few in China) polychromed on gold leaf. Here, in other rooms, is that strange singing bird described as living on a far snowy mountain, half dimpled girl, half feathered bird. And elsewhere sits the phoenix—no longer the brooding immortal of the Byodo-in but now a fabulous bird of paradise—all beak, claws, and primary colors.

As one turns a corridor corner, there is also the Sho-hojo, a garden said to be the work of the famous landscape artist Kobori Enshu (1579–1647). It stands there with the assurance of a theatrical decor. An expanse of sand from which, off center, springs an enchanted island of ancient pine, clipped privet, rounded stones, and curved bushes. To the left, balancing this rococo composition, is a large, dramatic rock fittingly called "Leaping Tiger." One thinks of Versailles, of the elegance that power can sometimes assume.

All of this is stylish and assured—the Momoyama style at its best. Later, however, in the ensuing Tokugawa period, this style was to degenerate into something approaching the arbitrary decoration of chinoiserie. One sees it at Nikko, in the Tokugawa mausoleum where every surface is carved and colored—alive with the Chinese children playing, with the Sleeping Cat, with the Three Monkeys. The effect is so vivid, and so vulgar, that we call it Seventeenth-Century Fox.

Another thought that intrudes itself is: how difficult it must be to dust. And, in so thinking, we reveal why the early Victorian tourists so loved Nikko. It was just like the what-nots, the shelves for bric-a-brac back home. Henry Adams, who had few good words for the country, had only praise for the place. He, like many another Victorian, loved the busy surface—as though the over-decorated could explain and excuse the sheer material worth of the place.

At Nanzen-ji, however, the Peach Mountain style named after Hideyoshi's gaudy palaces, now long destroyed, has not yet turned into Chinese Restaurant. Wandering the corridors and the courtyards, one is impressed by the firm ingenuity, the restrained lavishness, the tightly controlled imagination of the place. And one is also impressed by what all this must have cost. A new kind of materialism is on display in the art of the Momoyama—one that seeks to vindicate itself.

Tenryu-ji

天龍寺

When the emperor Go-Daigo died in 1338 after a difficult life—civil wars, exile—he did so holding a sutra in one hand and a sword in the other. This mixed message was seen as unsettling and the Zen priest Muso Kokushi told the new shogun, Ashikaga Takauji (1306–52), that the spirit should be appeased: a temple should be built on the site of the imperial villa where the late emperor had grown up, a scene of happier times.

Also, the shogun could thus redeem himself. This was much needed. How many had he murdered in his recent campaigns? asked the stern priest of the warrior, then answered his own question: "Fathers with no children, children with no fathers, families left homeless—we don't know how many there are."

That Muso could so speak to the highest military officer in the land indicates the moral authority held by the Zen sect and also the amount of political power which it had itself gathered.

Indeed, the shogun was already much worried about his salvation. He had gone to make a vow to the Kiyomizu-dera Kannon, promising that he would like to live in retirement to improve his prospects for the next world. So, building Tenryu-ji became one penance. Transcribing the entire Buddhist cannon was another. He commenced in the first month and finished, it is said, in the third. He did not himself do the copying, of course. Several hundred priests in various temples were put to work and he signed the results.

The new temple was part of a project which aimed at erecting temples in each of the sixty-six provinces. In scale it would surpass the Nara period construction project of provincial temples across the nation. These new temples would be known as Ankoku-ji, or temples to bring peace to the nation. That the former union had done nothing of the sort (and that for a time Buddhism was forbidden in the capital) was not recalled. Nor was there need to. The State could now control the Church.

Also, attractive as war proves, there comes a time when peace must break out. The battles of the northern and southern courts had ruined much of the country, and so Muso's was a definite move for peace, but one which could be accomplished only with the acquiescence of those who had caused the wars.

Consequently, the brave priest turned to his ruler and ordered him to thus "pray for the souls of those who died of their wounds in battle, the victims of war; and repent your sins for destroying these lives. Fear the retribution which you have incurred. Build this temple."

An occasion was discovered. It was soon said that the spirit of the dead emperor, carrying with it the souls of the slain, had been seen coming in the form of a fierce dragon from the roiling Oi River. Thus the creature indicated just where it wanted its new abode. The result was Tenryu-ji (Temple of the Heavenly Dragon), built not far from the river and on the site of an imperial villa where the dead emperor had spent his happy youth.

Naturally, the Tendai priests on Mount Hiei objected. Since Zen had, they said, long ago supported the states of the Song dynasty in China and since these had been ravaged by the Mongol hordes, this meant that Japanese Zen could not protect any state anywhere. Nonetheless construction continued, and around 1340 the shogun himself made a show of carrying some rocks about, and the dragon's home was declared complete.

Nonetheless the reigning emperor did not attend the 1344 dedication ceremonies. He was afraid to. Mass meetings had been held at Enryaku-ji and resolutions were passed reproving the court for dealing with Zen heretics—using such language as "demons masquerading as priests." The emperor thus thought it discrete not to appear on opening day but he did turn up the next, secretly. Though the imperial house actually sponsored the Zen sect it was still afraid openly to do so. So far as Enryaku-ji was concerned, the church still indeed controlled.

Later, in 1368, Tendai priests actually succeeded in getting the Zen monk Sosen exiled, and he was a friend not only of the imperial house but also of the shogun Yoshimitsu himself. Still, the laws of the Buddha were fading. With them much of the power of the imperial line also slipped away, at the very time

when the Ashikaga shoguns were building what we would now call new power bases.

Sansom tells an illustrative anecdote which speaks of imperial decline: a soldier was detected hunting while a royal edict said it was forbidden; he defended himself by saying that his commander had ordered him to and that since the law of his house was that disobedience was death, he preferred to disobey the emperor. Sure enough, he was merely banished.

The faith of Muso might have made him strong ("the chattering of three

卍

thousand monkeys does not alarm me" he said when he heard of the displeasure of the Mount Hiei monks) and the military position of the shogun might have lent him real power, but the influence of the imperial family was now so lessened that an emperor had to stay away from the inauguration of his father's temple. This caused much concern.

So did the cost. To raise more money a novel scheme was thought up. The shogunate commissioned a special ship known as the Tenryu Temple Boat (*Tenryu-ji-bune*) to engage in trade with China. The sponsors of this potentially lucrative scheme would contribute a set amount (a large one, some five thousand *kan* of copper cash) to the temple itself.

The boat sailed away from Japan in 1342 and safely returned the following year. It was the first Japanese ship authorized to sail to China following the aborted Mongol invasions of 1274 and 1281, and it was the first to return with all of those Chinese goods and ideas which were later to again so influence the country—this time with treasures from the Ming (1368–1644) rather those of the Tang and the Song dynasties.

Such funding also contributed to the affluence of Tenryu-ji itself. It became the first of the major Zen temples in the country and the largest Zen monastery in the western half of Kyoto. Though the temple was several times destroyed, funds to rebuild it were always found. Those buildings we now see are reconstructions dating from 1899.

The gardens, however, are more or less as they were. The Sogenchi Pond is still shaped like the Chinese ideograph which is pronounced *kokoro* in Japanese and which means untranslatably what the West has so thrust apart: "heart" and "mind."

The main garden was designed by Muso himself, who also made the famous moss garden at Saiho-ji. Incorporated into it are some biographical details from the life of Go-Daigo. The Tahoden is built in imitation of the palace where he had lived as a child, and around it stand cherry trees redolent of Yoshino, where he died. These were the so-called weeping-cherry trees (*shidare zakura*), whose drooping branches were thought to hang in mourning for the imperial dead.

At the base of the Ryumon waterfall the dragon, it is said, lies looking out over the garden which is intended to represent what the dragon well remembers, the country around Mount Horai, the ancient Chinese paradise.

All of this was brought about by the dedication and skill of Muso who in his famous treatise *Muchu Mondo* gave his secret of success. One was to go to a very high place and then, for once, see clearly. You will see that between you and the moon there is nothing at all.

Myoshin-ji

妙心寺

Outside the walls of Kyoto the great grid of imposed right-angled avenues turns into that maze of alleys which have always more naturally fitted both the Japanese landscape and the character of the Japanese people. Here, in the suburbs, remains something of the rustic native spirit of those upon whom the Chinese pattern had been so early set.

From early on, the rural temple with its massive gate sat in a field among the buckets and the clutter of the suburban farm. Visiting it, as seen in the poetry and paintings of the Heian period and later, were processions—city folk going out to rusticate.

We see them, brightly colored, lurching in their lumbering ox carts over the tilled fields, disporting themselves under the blossoms, having come from their proper straight avenues to the open labyrinths of lanes which still remain the natural home of these folk who built their houses under the hems, as it were, of this imposing but imported Chinese garment.

Sei Shonagon, seeking solace during the rounds of her days, all circumscribed in rituals intended to keep the aristocracy busy, found especially delightful the week of winter when the courtiers went out to pick the young herbs which had sprouted green under snow. She writes in her pillow book, the *Makura no Soshi,* that it was amusing to see their excitement when such plants were found growing near the palace, a place where no one expected them.

卍

The Japanese have made much of nature. So have others but none perhaps

with more dedication. Nature was early and permanently woven into habit and language. Not only were the spatial facts of spring fields and autumn orchards rendered obligatory in writing and in talk, but also the temporal facts of rain and sun and the daily temperature were so ingrained that even now— so late—it is still impermissible to leave out of note or fax or e-mail some reference to the weather and its possible ability to alarm or delight.

What, one wonders, could have so motivated so early such an enormous concern. Perhaps, just as the Egyptians so loved living that they constructed the pyramids, those titanic containers of the dead, so the Japanese, aware of gossamer life, of this short respite before the setting of the sun of late summer, enameled onto all their words and thoughts these colors of eternity—the world of nature which lives but to die and dies but to live.

卍

One such rural temple was Myoshin-ji, but over the years as the city grew it lost its rustic air and eventually became a complex of temples and, like the medieval cathedrals of Europe, a center of learning. It was here that the retired emperor Hanazono (who had reigned from 1309 to 1318) studied his Buddhism.

He had trained under the Master Shuho Myocho, the Zen master now popularly known as Daito Kokushi, the founder of Daitoku-ji, and he had been diligent. Now, after some time having practiced the disciplines of Zen, he believed that enlightenment might be his, and so wrote his master a verse— the *toki no gosho* which disciples wrote to their *roshi* when they believed they were ready.

In it the cloistered emperor said that for twenty years he had persevered and that lately, in this coming summer, he had begun to believe he might finally have been successful. He just ate his meals and drank his tea, he said. He seemed to live in a world where everything was quite clear but wouldn't his teacher please test him. To this, Master Shuho answered by addressing him as distinguished priest and added that he had already been tested.

With such a diploma from such an authority the retired emperor decided to turn his own detached palace into a home for Zen teachings, and thus the Shobozan Myoshin-ji (The Temple of the True Dharma and the Miraculous Heart) came into being. To serve as founder and high priest, Hanazono chose

Kanzan Egen (1277–1360), the only teacher whom Shuho thought worthy of such a position.

A man of elegant simplicity, Kanzan was noted for a somewhat luxurious artlessness. His robes were expertly woven from a fiber made from the common wisteria. On his desk was nothing literary or priestly. It contained only a receptacle into which he put his letters from the unhappy emperor Go-Daigo, Hanazono's successor.

Yet he was also very strict. Holding that study was not enough, he said that a master must be so rigorous as to approximate the transience of life itself. Only in this way—by enduring the worst as it were—could progress be made. He must have been a terror and a salvation to his student. One of them, his own nephew, he kicked out more than twenty times. The perserverant lad always returned, though to what eventual end history does not tell us.

Perhaps, like Spinoza a few hundred years later, he understood that everything happens through necessity—and that once one achieves this embracing perception, one is close to harmony and happiness—by-products of what Zen calls enlightenment. This late seventeenth-century Dutch Buddhist wrote that our passions prevent our achieving this harmony and happiness, and yet we can still come to realize that everything is related, that everything is one.

The fact that Myoshin-ji was run like a very strict religious school might account for its layout, odd among the big Zen temples, though the customs of Zen construction were followed faithfully enough. It is enormous but not compact in that linear way of most Japanese temple complexes: telling a story and starting with the fact of the grand front gate.

It covers nearly seven acres, has its great Sanmon, its *butsuden,* lecture hall, and so on. But it also then extends to form a small city with a main street, side alleys, all in neat rows, dormitories systematically arranged on the east and west sides of the larger buildings. It is like a university town, a campus. Even today it contains nearly sixty subtemples and has nearly four thousand affiliated temples throughout the country.

Eventually, however, it lost its authority and came under the control of Nanzen-ji, its more powerful neighbor. Still later this entire college town was destroyed in the Onin Wars. Restored and rebuilt by its ninth abbot, Sekko Sojin in the late fifteenth-century, it remains an important branch of the Rinzai sect of Zen, still filled with teaching priests and earnest acolytes.

And right next door is the hill, Narabigaoka, where Yoshida Kenko wrote *Essays in Idleness.* Though his house faced Ninna-ji, he often used to listen to the great bell of Myoshin-ji. "The sound of the bell is precisely the tone of *oshiki,*" he wrote (this being standard pitch used to tune the instruments of the imperial orchestra, the *gagaku*). "The pitch naturally rises and falls according to the temperature . . . so this tone evokes the atmosphere of transience."

Some commentators, however, have said that he must have meant another bell since the original and ancient Myoshin-ji bell, said to be the oldest inscribed bell in Japan (the twenty-third day of the fourth month of 698), had disappeared long before.

Real or not, the sense of evanescence, the slow decay of the mighty stroke in the air of an evening as its vesper roar flattens to a whisper, a mere vibration, then silence—this is real.

Kinkaku-ji

金閣寺

 The Ashikaga shogun Yoshimitsu (1358–1408), of the ruling house which had set up its hegemony in 1336, having consolidated his reign, abducted in favor of his nine-year-old son. Retired, he took over the Kitayama Mansion of the Saionji family and turned it into a villa for himself, in the process adding a number of buildings, including the Reliquary—a three-storied tower structure, overlooking the Kyoko-ike (Mirror Pond)—later popularly known as the Golden Temple.

This he must have accomplished with a sense of relief. His reign had been much criticized, particularly his efforts at trade with Ming-period China where, said the critics, he had accepted a tributary relationship—though all that Yoshimitsu had intended was simple trade relations.

Now safely an ex-shogun, he continued much as he had before. In the words of one commentator "he carried to an extreme the parvenu ostentation which marked the behavior of the military class when it found itself the master of Kyoto." Though he exacted all-but-imperial honors he had to content himself with ceremonial gestures because, like the Kamakura shoguns before him, he had become but a nominal ruler—the great feudatories being controlled by the major *daimyo* who exercised the real authority.

Nevertheless, this retreat was for Yoshimitsu what Byodo-in had been for Michinaga: the expression of a power which, as Herbert Plutschow finely phrased it, "was understood to transcend the temporal." Indeed, the building we now know as the Golden Pavilion was intended as a metaphor.

The pillars extend the structure itself over the pond, which suggests that the place of proper worship is between heaven and earth. It was also otherwise built to conform to descriptions of the Western Paradise of the Buddha Amida, and to embody the harmony which ought exist between heaven and art.

At the same time, of course, it also suggested that this paradise could be found on earth, and that if it were built by someone of the taste and discernment of Yoshimitsu this might even surpass the celestial version. One of Yoshimitsu's ministers apparently thought so. He is said to have remarked that "the beauty of the Pavilion is superior to even Amida's Western Paradise."

And so it was, continues Plutschow, that "the Golden Pavilion, like other temples built by political figures, symbolizes legitimized political power—legitimized, that is, by heavenly mandate."

Originally, perhaps, the place appeared even more heavenly. There is some evidence that it was once entirely surrounded by the pond on the edge of which it now perches. Guests arrived by pleasure boat. Such indeed was the mode of the emperor Go-Komatsu when he, in 1408, condescended to visit the shogun Yoshimitsu, an event thought to be the first time a ruler had visited anyone outside the noble court circles. The boating party was probably splendid—though brief since the pond is quite small—and the celebrations concluded with a fine Noh performance.

This drama was but one of the aesthetic indulgences or ostentations of the retired ruler. He pursued this expensive hobby because he so appreciated the artistry of one Kan'ami (1333–84), a Shinto priest from Kasuga Shrine turned actor, or because—a reason bandied at the time and since—he was taken with the charms of the priest's son, the teenaged Zeami (1363–1444). In any event the Noh drama flourished and little Zeami became the famed author of many plays as well as that actor's guide, the *Kadensho.*

Sansom has characterized Kinkaku-ji, both temple and its grounds, as a work of deliberate aestheticism. The pavilion is designed and placed so as to harmonize with a landscape garden, itself the product of the most conscious artifice. Together the structure and the garden formed an integral whole, and the shape of the building was of no greater importance than the distribution of the rocks.

Even today the care with which the pond was created is apparent. At water's edge small rocks and bushes are used, while behind larger elements are introduced, gradually extending the boundaries and making the place seem much larger than it is—even Mount Kinugasa is eventually included as

borrowed scenery. Along the shoreline the many peninsulas and small islands conceal the real size of the water and make it suggest something more vast.

Architecturally, the place was praised from the start. It perfectly mated, it was said, the residential and Buddhist styles. The first two stories were in the *shinden-zukuri* style of domestic architecture and even had folding shutters just as high-class houses did. The third story consisted of an eighteen-foot-square apartment built in the Zen style. This further reflected, it was also said, the tastes of Yoshimitsu who in himself harmonized both secular and ecclesiastical demands. Here were all of the comforts of the court and at the same time a secluded privacy where religious meditation was encouraged. The effect was eclectic to an extreme—religion and worldly concerns were combined, as were frugality and luxury.

After Yoshimitsu's death, the villa was turned into a Zen temple and was called Rokuon-ji, the designation of Golden Temple coming later. Yet, from the first, the interior of the third floor was covered with gold leaf and the outside of the entire structure was painted with gold lacquer. It must have been the most expensive building yet constructed in the country.

One might wonder why, if the desire was an expression of oneness with nature, of simple retreat, of frugal and lonely pleasure, the building should be covered with expensive gold leaf. This has troubled those scholars down the ages who bothered to consider the matter. One explanation is that ostentation was not the intent, though it turned out to be the result.

The reason was that the gold was metaphorical. The sage Kobo Daishi had said so in his *Sango Shiiki:* "There are no fixed heavens or hells . . . if you do good, gold and silver pavilions immediately appear." Their appearance was thus not an admission of tastelessness but an exhibition of virtue.

The pavilion was also from the first a reliquary in which holy objects were to be exhibited—among them, eventually, a statue of Yoshimitsu himself. At the same time, the fact that this blinding building was also apparently made of money gave the structure an ambivalence which has echoed through the ages.

Many visitors have noticed that to properly appreciate the beauty of the building, and to cut the dazzle, one should look rather at its reflection in Kyoko-ike in front of it. Among those who recommended this was the poet-aesthete Ishikawa Jozan. On the night of the fourteenth day of the eighth month of the *kigai* year of the Genna period (September 8, 1623), he crossed

the city from his Shisen-do in order to view the moon over Kinkaku-ji. There he looked at the shining pavilion, then lowered his gaze and wrote of the more wondrous sight of its reflection glittering in the water's depths.

And well over three hundred years later the novelist Yukio Mishima would write: "On the other side of the water the Golden Temple revealed its façade in the declining sun [and] cast a perfect shadow on the surface of the pond, where the duckweed and the leaves from water plants were floating. The shadow was more beautiful than the building itself."

In this celebrated novel, the 1956 *Kinkaku-ji* (The Temple of the Golden Pavilion), Mishima gave further indications of ambivalence of the place. The author writes: "It sat there in utter silence, like some elegant but useless piece of furniture, with the antique gold foil of its interior perfectly protected by the lacquer of the summer sun that doubled the outer walls. Great, empty display shelves placed before the burning green of the forest. What ornamental objects could one put on such shelves?"

The young acolyte who is describing the place to us saw that: "The Golden Temple stood before me, towered before me, like some terrifying pause in a piece of music, like some resonant silence."

It was just such an acolyte who, perhaps equally impressed by the ambivalent beauty of the place, burned it down in 1950 and thus inspired the Mishima novel. And so the structure over five centuries and a half old, built in 1397, just two years after Chaucer had completed *The Canterbury Tales,* disappeared with all of its treasures, including the statue of Yoshimitsu, carrying off into the spark-strewn sky a true vision of evanescence.

Since then the position of the Golden Pavilion has become even more ambivalent. Naturally, it was reconstructed almost at once and was put on display still smelling of cut wood and fresh lacquer. But it was, of course, not the same building. Westerners still hold this against it.

In his magisterial *Kyoto: A Contemplative Guide,* 1964, Gouveneur Mosher refused to write about it at all. "To those who wish I had included the Golden Pavilion, I recommend the Silver . . . when choosing between the two, one must consider their respective dates: Silver, 1483; Gold, 1955 (and it looks it)."

Yet this fact of its history is otherwise merely thirty years later almost forgotten. The place is again a National Treasure. People come and look as though at the real thing. And in a certain way, it is.

The great shrine at Ise is destroyed every twenty years and a precise replica is erected in its place. This process known as *shikinen sengu* (periodic transfer) has been going on five times a century for over a millennium and so any idea of an original is lost in time. It is, after all, the immortality of the concept that is important and not its outward manifestation.

This truth is still acknowledged in Japan. It is the concept of *ie,* not the "house" itself that is important, and when Mishima killed himself shouting for the emperor he did not mean Hirohito—he meant the concept: emperorhood. The essence of things is emphasized rather than the material reality.

The acolyte hero of the novel similarly ponders. "If I burn down the Golden Temple, I told myself, I shall be doing something that will have great educational value. For it will teach people that it is meaningless to infer indestructibility by analogy. They will learn that the mere fact of the Golden Temple's having continued to exist, of its having continued to stand for five hundred and fifty year confers no guaranty upon it whatsoever."

In burning the temple the acolyte confers upon it the transience which its very golden appearance had seemed to refuse. And so, since all is transient and since evanescence is truth acknowledged, Kinkaku-ji, now just forty years-old, a wall newly cracked by the 1995 Great Hanshin Earthquake, still stands.

Ginkaku-ji

銀閣寺

The famous "Temple of the Silver Pavilion" is more properly known as Jisho-ji, so named after the posthumous name of Yoshimasa, the eighth Ashikaga shogun (1435–90). It was he who sponsored the construction and the grounds surrounding it, and who came most to typify the Muromachi period, the most turbulent period in Japanese history.

He began planning his retreat in 1474 even before—as was now customary with shogunal as well as imperial authority—he retired. Though not yet forty years old, Yoshimasa, like shoguns before and after him, had had quite enough of this troubled world and longed to get away from politics and into something more restful: tea tasting, flower viewing, moon gazing, incense smelling, poetry contests—the aesthetic pursuits. A whole round of tempered pleasure awaited him.

He had ample reason. Things had gone very badly from the first. His older brother, heir incumbent, had died and the thirty-year-old Yoshimasa was thrust into the shogunal seat. He had no talent for ruling and the Ashikaga hegemony was in any event coming apart. As he himself wrote in a private letter: "The *daimyo* do as they please and do not follow orders. That means there can be no government." And that meant that he would no longer attempt to rule.

Originally he had intended to have his younger brother take over after his resignation, with one of the Hosokawa family acting as regent. But directly after this decision, Yoshimasa's wife gave birth to a son and began setting up this infant as shogun, availing herself of the power of the Yamana family.

These two feuding families were joined by others and this resulted in that decade-long chain of battles known as the Onin War, during which Kyoto itself was largely destroyed and the reputation of the Ashikaga shogunates fell lower yet.

Even before this, however, both misfortune and mismanagement had been so extreme that during Yoshimasa's reign the government was thirteen times obliged to issue orders for a general cancellation of debt. By 1477 the Onin War was finally over, but fighting continued in most of the provinces. The imperial house was bankrupt and the Ashikagas were powerless. As the central government collapsed so did all civic order and by 1500 the entire country was at odds.

It was from all of this that Yoshimasa desired respite. He had had enough of war and he wanted peace, even if it was but an artificial one which he himself would construct and maintain. His tastes were courtly. Like the Taira before them, the Ashikagas were fond of imperial pursuits. He would make himself a private world, guarded, entry strictly restricted, where cut off from his country as well as from his times he could devote himself to a life measured only by the demands of courtly aesthetics.

In this he had precedent. His grandfather, Yoshimitsu, had done something much like this when he constructed Kinkaku-ji. He had retired and lived to an aesthetic old age, still busying himself, untroubled by the turmoil elsewhere. If the grandfather had a golden pavilion then the grandson could have a silver one.

Having in 1474 retired to his retreat, Yoshimasa and his circle savored Song paintings and porcelains, the precious adjuncts of the tea ceremony. They discussed the merits of calligraphy, or composed suitable verses while looking at the moon over the garden. These activities were, like most courtly exercises, antiquarian. They looked backward to Heian predecessors and created a peaceful aesthetic world though outside raged the Sengoku Wars.

Also, he, like his grandfather, would decree that after his death the place would turn ecclesiastical and become a proper temple. Yoshimitsu had chosen the Zen sect so this is what his Yoshimasa did as well. Zen was aristocratic and it was much concerned with the arts. And thankfully it did not have the popular appeal of such mass religions as that superstitious old-fashioned Tendai sect or the Jodo Shinshu with its vulgar Pure Land beliefs and its chanting hordes.

Thus it was fitting that when it came time (1480) to build, Yoshimasa chose to dispossess just such a Tendai temple complex—a venerable compound thought to have been built in the later Heian period. Though the Ashikaga court viewed that era as a kind of golden age and now grew nostalgic over those good old days, this did not prevent the retired shogun from knocking down most of the ancient structures in order to make room for his own.

And since this location was in a corner of the capital known as Higashiyama, on the eastern side of Kyoto, the art associated with Yoshimasa and his court came to be known as Higashiyama culture, in contrast to Kitayama culture, named after the location of Kinkaku-ji, in the northern hills of Kyoto.

The Higashiyama style was noted for its luxuriance, elegance and expense. It was the high baroque which was eventually superseded by the rococo extravagances of the late Momoyama period. Something like its early sturdiness can be found by analogy to the style of the Tudor dynasty that was just at this time being formed: the buildings of both are plainly built, highly decorated, and full of that ostentatious display everywhere associated with power.

The pavilion itself, however, was fittingly a copy of the Ruri-den at the Saiho-ji, a building completed nearly two centuries earlier. This fit nicely with the antiquarian tastes of Yoshimasa and his circle. When the structure was completed in 1483, he moved in at once and thus perhaps never got around to covering it with the intended silver foil which would have justified its later popular name. Rather than completing the pavilion in the manner intended, he commissioned other structures (most of the originals now destroyed) and was still building when he himself died seven years later.

He also obtained the services of the noted aestheticians of his time all of whom took the last two syllables of their names from the first two of Amida's: Noami, his son Geiami, and his grandson Soami—a poet-priest, a flower arranger, an incense master, and an aesthete of many parts.

It was Soami who designed some of these buildings, including the Togu-do used by Yoshimasa for his devotions, in which there was a small chamber now considered (as are several others in the city) to be the true prototype of the classic tea-room.

The retired shogun himself is given credit for the design of the garden—both sections of it. The first part remains noted for its many expensive stones,

such being then as now indicative of the wealth and taste of their owners. Arranged around the border of the Kinkyochi (Brocade Mirror Pond), most of these are tastefully hidden by trees and moss, indicating a pleasing lack of ostentation in the wealthy owner and advertising the fact that the garden at Saiho-ji, the so-called "Moss Garden," had been one of its models.

Here Yoshimasa's guests could stroll and come upon this planned view or that controlled perspective. There was the White Crane Island, named after that bird which symbolizes the posthumous longevity enjoyed by the inhabitants of Horai-san, Island of the Blessed Immortals; there was also its counterpart, the Immortal Hermit's Isle, and a bridge made of a single stone eight feet in length known as the Dragon's-Back Bridge. And there was the Sengetsusen, or Moon-Washing Spring, so named because Yoshimasa, it is said, would sit and watch the water wash away the reflections of the moon. Most of the attractions of this garden were also picturesque references to places famous in Chinese and Japanese literature and thus Yoshimasa's well-read friends could make suitable comments indicative of their appreciation.

The second part is not of this ambulatory (*kayushiki*) variety. It is *karesansui,* a dry garden intended to be simply looked at while standing or sitting. This consists of two large areas of sand. One is carefully combed and is known as Ginsadan (Silver Sand Beach) while the other, mounded and truncated, is Kogetsudai. The first is thought to be shaped after a celebrated lake near Hangzhou in China.

There is some scholarly disagreement as to just what mountain is being referred to in the second shape, however, though the popular imagination has it that it is a view of Mount Fuji as seen from Sagami Bay. If so, this is then a graceful reference to the former stronghold of the Minamoto shoguns, the military city of Kamakura from whence just such a view is sometimes available.

Commentators agree, however, that both of these sand shapes were religious metaphors. Enlightenment in Zen was often represented as moonlight over water—it is the moon which makes the water visible, and vice-versa, since the water reflects the image. But the sand shapes were also meant to assist the various imaginings indulged in during Yoshimasa's moon-viewing parties.

The ornamental sand pile, the Kogetsudai, is known as the Moon-Facing Mound. This is because here Yoshimasa and his guests awaited the rising of the full moon. It was also here that on December 28, 1487, that the ex-shogun wrote a celebrated verse about his waiting under the dark hill for the full moonrise, and how his longing grew as the sky slowly lightened.

The dark hill was a mountain spur which cut off the view of the moon and thus enhanced the suspense in so artistic a manner. The hill was consequently given a name: Tsukimachiyama (Moon-Waiting Mountain). The poem itself was seen as an expression of the subtlety that the anticipation of beauty may be even more pleasing than its actuality. Even more subtle were the gatherings when there was no moon at all, for then everything had to be imagined. This called for great sensibility, gratified in the person of the shogun himself. At least this was the opinion of Yoshimasa's secretary who elsewhere often spoke of his master as "that man of incomparable taste."

Whether either of these sand shapes were ever looked at during the daytime is debatable. In this century, however, that is the only time they are ever seen. Hence today they are found very "modern" looking and these abstract-seeming shapes, are as pleasingly incongruous to the modern eye as Pei's glass pyramid in the Louvre, and as admired.

The Togu-do (just east of the reconstructed Hon-do) is the original structure. This, it is said, is where Yoshimasa lived and held his artistic parties. There was not only moon viewing but also incense burning. Here the participants competed in guessing the names of the rare and expensive woods and powders being burned. Scores were kept and prizes given. The separate room where this took place itself perished amid eventual conflagrations, but one may imagine the cultivated reek, perfumes darkening the sky, as the massed sandalwood, bay, and myrrh burned and bubbled away. It is now, like so much else, rebuilt—in the words of the guide—as "an exact facsimile, reconstructed from old plans in the possession of the temple."

At Ginkaku-ji it is the pavilion, however, which attracts the most interest. The original building, it stands there, ostentatiously refined—so much more so than Kinkaku-ji, a gaudy seventy-year-old when Ginkaku-ji was being built. Indeed, it is so simple that one authority (George Sansom) has called it an insignificant structure, simple to the verge of insipidity.

Even so, it remains as an expression of the taste of Yoshimasa and his circle. Architecturally, it is a compromise between the old religious style (the windows are in the arch shape associated with Zen) and the new style of *shoin-zukuri,* sets of rooms to live in which specialists regard as the forerunner of the modern Japanese house.

Here Yoshimasa sat and perhaps meditated. He had much to meditate upon. Now ruin was complete and riot had spread throughout the country: the Sengoku Wars constituted more than one hundred years of strife. It was the consequences of this that Yoshimasa had wished to avoid in his cultured retreat.

Here at his hermitage, he said, he recalled the glories of the past as the moon slowly sank in the western sky. Penning this lyric he gave himself up to contemplation and neglected his shogunal duties, allowing his country ruin and his people misery. It is no wonder then that as late as 1877 Kyoto people used to go to Ginkaku-ji and give five yen apiece to be allowed to beat the statue of the Ashikaga shogun which had been erected there.

Higashi Hongan-ji

 The two Hongan-ji, east and west, were originally one. Upon the death of Shinran in 1262, venerable at the age of ninety, the emperor Kameyama gave his old *shishin-den* to the order (Jodo Shinshu) and ten years later a temple was built to hold the holy ashes and the whole complex was properly named. Hongan-ji means "Temple of the Primal Vow" and celebrates Shinran's belief that one recitation was (contrary to Honen's repetitions) quite enough. All further repetition of the formula, he wrote, being only praise, pleasant but useless.

Over the years the sect and its main temple flourished but always had to contend, as did everyone else, with enmity of Enryaku-ji. Finally in 1470 the quarrelsome monks from Mount Hiei had the priest Rennyo, eighth in his line (1415–99), officially expelled. They had burned down Hongan-ji itself and they chased the unfortunate priest out of the city.

Rennyo went north—to Omi, Echizen, Yamashina—where his evangelism had successful results. His new followers formed communities, challenged the local authorities, and even took a new name. They called themselves the Ikko (Single-Minded) sect, a name based upon a phrase much used by Rennyo (*Ikko Isshin,* "one direction, one heart"). However, the sect, escaping the founder's control, took to methods that were so militant, and to uprisings so extensive, that it was soon dubbed *Ikko Ikki,* which might be translated as "Fanatical Uprising."

The local *daimyo* made what use they could of this militant group, to play one partisan sect off against another or to suppress the risings of the hungry peasants. In 1532 the Nichiren party (supported by the Hosokawa family) attacked an Ikko stronghold. The reason was religious dissent and the object

was the securing of true Buddhism. By 1537 Rennyo's sect had gotten the government to suppress the followers of Nichiren's party. In this case, however, the militants were unsuccessful. A great battle took place in Kyoto, and all twenty-one Hokke temples were destroyed with many priests and followers slaughtered and, as so often occurred, dark smoke ascended to the clear Kyoto sky.

Behind blind faith, purposeful politics were now plainly visible. As Marguerite Yourcenar has said of completely different religious wars: "By now the two warring religions were, as almost always the case with rival ideologues, nothing but the pretext or the disguise of the violent and the ambitious, a means of rousing mass hysteria, a way of sanctifying the arms of cunning in the eyes of the foolish and the dull."

That Buddhists of whatever sect could revive themselves to wield such power indicated a new weakness of the central government. Indeed, the Buddhist church by the end of the fifteenth century was close to regaining the empire of Japan for itself. That it did not, says Sansom, was because the church was as much a prey to schism as the shogunate was prone to factions.

These various squabbles lead to the calamity of the Onin War. The ostensible reason for this famous folly was, as we have seen, the reigning Ashikaga shogun Yoshimasa's squabbling over succession rights with his own family and then with the heads of rival families. Soon the decade-long war broke out, one which brought no advantage to either side and laid waste to Kyoto, ending only with the exhaustion of the combatants.

It was a full scale war with extensive results. In 1477, battles still raging, the emperor Go-Tsuchimikado sought refuge in the shogun's palace and then in 1500 died on the throne because he was too poor to retire. After that his body was left for six weeks because there was no money for his funeral.

The succeeding emperor, Go-Kashiwabara, reigned for two whole decades before the funds were found for his enthronement ceremony. The palace had by then been destroyed. Living in a hut, the emperor was reduced to selling what amounted to his autograph, specimens of imperial calligraphy, for money. Nor did things much improve. When Oda Nobunaga's troops occupied the capital and the new emperor Ogimachi held a welcoming banquet, it consisted only of noodle soup. Not, people said, that the new warlord deserved better fare.

Oda was a petty *daimyo* who had through expeditious treaties with other families, and a series of well-coordinated attacks against common enemies, reached a position of eminence. It was he to whom the emperor Ogimachi had turned in his efforts to pacify the land; he whom Ashikaga Yoshiaki had asked for support in order to secure the succession of his brother, the shogun Yoshiteru. And it was he who would eventually rise to the highest honors of the land and begin that grand, creative, repressive reorganization of the land which the Tokugawa family would complete.

Oda was also unpopular. He had militantly forced the populace of Kyoto to welcome him; when he needed stones to build his castle on the shores of Lake Biwa he ordered the heads from the stone Buddhas removed and used; and when the people of north Kyoto could not pay the taxes he had levied, he burned down that entire section. But he did, as we have seen, do something about Enryaku-ji.

Though the monks of Mount Hiei had not been popular favorites within the city, still, they were nonetheless a part of the local scene, which the Oda was not. Their destruction in 1571, along with their temple citadel, was thus viewed as a calamity. The poet Sakunen commemorated the ruin with a poem that spoke of all the temples great and small sent swirling up in the smoke, the waters of the lake below growing warm with the conflagration even as the embers of three thousand temples grew cold. When Oda was assassinated in 1582 Kyoto was pleased.

卍

The unification was then taken over by one of Oda's generals, Toyotomi Hideyoshi. This warlord—Oda's second-in-command and born in the ranks— had need of a traditional pomp that could add a needed luster to his origins. So he set about reconstructing the city into something resembling the imperial capital it had once been.

He also, like Kammu, having seen what power the church could wield even in its latter days, took care to restrict the influence of the temples. He particularly placed the hostile Nichiren and Jodo sects where they could be watched. At the same time he himself made religious gestures. One of his projects was the great Buddha which he ordered cast. This gave him a reason for his now-famous sword hunt of 1585 which allowed him for holy reasons to confiscate all privately owned weapons under the slogan: "Give Iron to the Buddha." General Hideyoshi said that "back in the old days of the emperor Shomu it took two decades to cast the Nara Buddha. I will do it in five years." And so he did.

He also erected its big Hoko-ji temple as well. Neither the temple nor its statue lasted as long as Nara's, however, because an earthquake toppled both in 1596, not even ten years after their completion. Along with them went the infamous Mimizuka, the mound composed of the moldering ears taken from those slain during Hideyoshi's grandiose but unsuccessful attack on Korea— whole heads being too bulky to bring all the way back.

Since he was busy with all his other projects it was not until 1591 that Hideyoshi had the opportunity to arrange for the Hongan-ji to return home, as it were. Much was made of the move. The huge pillars needed for the founder's hall were dragged in procession through the streets, but since not enough ropes were available, local temples were asked to help. Hearing of the problem, "female devotees, without hesitation," says the official pamphlet, "cut off their hair to weave massive ropes."

These, called *kezuna,* were fifty-three in number, and the largest (again

information from the pamphlet) was 367 feet in length, over a foot in circumference, and weighed over two thousand pounds. It—or one like it—is still on display, an oddly fierce-looking object, under glass, dusty and frayed, but indisputably a hair rope.

No sooner was the temple up, however, than the sect itself was given over to inner rivalry. After the death in 1592 of Kennyo, his eldest son Kyonyo was appointed. Since this child had once been disowned by his departed father, however, his younger brother Junyo took advantage of this fact and put himself up for the post.

Kennyo had been much opposed to Oda Nobunaga, as had the new warlord, so when Hideyoshi took over, he decided to beautify Hongan-ji—perhaps largely because the dead warlord had so disliked it. Hideyoshi even gave the temple a Noh stage (still there) from his own palace, the luxurious Juraku-dai. In addition, he decided to recognize the younger brother. This meant that Kyonyo, the eldest son, was forced into retirement.

Kyonyo, however, was no stranger to intrigue by this time and realized that the true power lay no longer with Hideyoshi but with Tokugawa Ieyasu, the warlord who would shortly replace him. It was thus Kyonyo who was cloistered together with Ieyasu on the very eve of the climactic Battle of Sekigahara in 1600 that elevated the Tokugawa family to the highest power.

Nevertheless, it is probably not true that the two made a compact which would have enabled Ieyasu to divide and subjugate the True Pure Land sect's adherents. It is possible, though, that there was some agreement to the effect that when Ieyasu came to power he would do something about all this rivalry within the sect. In any event, Ieyasu built in 1603 another, grander temple, just east of Hongan-ji. This became Higashi (East) Hongan-ji and Kyonyo was installed as its abbot.

Though the shogunate did not officially recognize the establishment as an independent branch of Jodo Shinshu until 1619, Kyonyo was in full power and so he remained for a time. His temple had managed to survive the vicissitudes of three warlords, each one different, each one dangerous.

The dangers were apparent and the differences were indicated in a saying of the period:

Nobunaga says, "Cuckoo, if you don't sing, I will kill you."
Hideyoshi says, "Cuckoo, if you don't sing, I'm going to make you."
Ieyasu says, "Cuckoo, if you don't sing, I'll just wait until you do."

Still, Hongan-ji split in two was only half as powerful as it had been before. In addition, the new temple did not prosper. The buildings were all destroyed in the great Kyoto fire of 1783, then were burned down again in 1823, in 1854, and once again in 1864. The sad later history of the temple, indeed of all temples, might be seen as symbolic of the decline of Buddhism.

The *mappo no yo* proved to be the latter days of the law indeed, and the collapse of this religion as a political power occurred with the unification of the country. Nobunaga and Hideyoshi had broken the power of the church and the legislation of Ieyasu ensured its continuing impotence.

A result of all this is that Higashi Hongan-ji does not have the architectural authority of Nishi Hongan-ji. However the grand founder's hall, completed in 1895, does have the distinction of being, along with the Daibutsuden at Nara's Todai-ji, one of the world's largest wooden buildings. Also, claims the pamphlet, anxious to make the most of what it has, this great barn contains nine hundred twenty-seven *tatami* mats and, on the roof, nearly one hundred seventy-six thousand tiles. These must be constantly renewed and each of the faithful are invited to sign one of these with their name and address. Thus, for a not inconsiderable sum, one may become a part of the house of Buddha.

Higashi Hongan-ji is still much in the business of saving souls though its rate of success can be nothing like it was in the days of Shinran. Perhaps this is the reason it has modernized its teaching. "Let Us Discover the Significance of Birth and the Joy of Living" proclaims a billboard outside the temple precincts. This banal generality is far from the stunning particularity of the *nembutsu*. The latter is a personal shout of exaltation; the former was recently formulated by a committee.

Higashi Hongan-ji, still anxious to proclaim its excellence over its larger rival temple, has long claimed to hold the remains of Shinran the founder. But so does Nishi Hongan-ji. Each indeed has a such a mausoleum, but neither has the holy ashes. These are at Nishi Otani.

Shisen-do

An enforced peace was the result of the victory of the Tokugawa shogunate. It now held one quarter of the country's agricultural land and it administrated the major cities of Kyoto, Osaka, and Nagasaki. Much of the remaining land was divided into areas (*han*) and distributed among the *daimyo*, both those originally loyal to the Tokugawas and those who later were persuaded to be.

Intensely conservative, the Tokugawa shogunate was concerned only with the status quo, and exerted a real pressure on the individual to conform to rigid rules based upon what was seen as virtuous Confucian behavior. Loyalty was paramount. Ieyasu was fittingly made shogun the very year that Queen Elizabeth I died (1603) for he, too, was excessively concerned with fidelity. There was nonetheless an amount of dissent and consequently, in Japan as in England, a number of executions and exiles.

Among the latter was the exile of Ishikawa Jozan (1583–1672) a fairly high-ranking samurai who was put under house-arrest and eventually dismissed by Ieyasu for opposing the wishes of that dictator by seeking to retire from the military life and take up residence at the Buddhist temple complex of Myoshin-ji, where he had gone to school.

At the age of thirty-three Jozan, having become a *ronin*, a masterless samurai, and having nowhere else to go, now returned against the expressed wishes of his ex-lord to Myoshin-ji, and there devoted himself to the Buddhist life.

In this he had ample precedent. Kumagai Naozane had, for whatever reason, retired to Komyo-ji, Kamo no Chomei had retired to his "hut" which

he wrote about it in his diary, the *Hojoki,* and Yoshida Kenko had gone to live on the hill in front of Ninna-ji where he penned his famous *Essays in Idleness.*

At Myoshin-ji, Jozan devoted himself not to the Buddha but to the study of the classics. The step from the sword of the Japanese samurai to the Chinese brush of the sage was not, however, all that big. Zen Buddhism had demonstrated that these two were not incompatible. And Jozan was also (given his position) particularly taken with Chinese notion of the scholar who looks on but does not partake. Indeed, as J. Thomas Rimer has said: "The idea of a cultivated gentleman living inside and outside society at the same time provided a perfect model for the life that Jozan had been seeking."

He had himself early begun writing poetry, as did many warriors of his class, and he continued this interest while in the temple compounds. Now, however, his poetry was no longer that of the lyrical samurai. It began to accord with that of the Chinese *wenren.* These poets, the name to be rendered *bunjin* in Japanese, gracefully retired, removed themselves from all worldly concerns, indeed, despised social involvement and considered gentlemanly detachment a mark of an artist. The term is often translated as "literary artist," and delicate brush strokes and pale colors constitute a description of the object painted, a studied and objective realism.

There was in these paintings the Zen-like thought that in this deliberate non-involvement one is closer to the nature of things. The *bunjin* school of flower arrangement, for example, insists that you impose no ideas of your own. Rather, simply observe your materials, this stem, that branch, and they will tell you what to do.

Behind this is a rejection of the idea of self, one perhaps derived from Zen, but to our eyes equally if accidentally close to that more secularly stated by David Hume a century later. This self is but a collection of different perceptions, always in movement—a kind of theater, thought Hume. And as for personal identity, he would have agreed with Zen that there is only this succession of thoughts which keeps man in a continued state of change—one in which you cannot say that this is mine nor this is me.

Jozan became one of the earliest *bunjin,* writing classical verse in Chinese, living a life aloof from common concerns, cultivating only like-minded friends, such as the Confucian scholar and philosopher Fujiwara no Seika, his elder by some twenty years and the perfect example of the cultivated recluse.

What he needed now was, like Kamo no Chomei and Yoshida Kenko, a place in which to practice his cultivated seclusion. The obligations of his world (his duties, his sick mother, his not having enough money) were such, however, that it was not until 1641, at the age of fifty-eight, that Jozan was ready to build his retreat.

This is the Shisen-do, the House of the Poet-Hermits (or, more grandly, The Hall of the Poetry Immortals), an elegant little dwelling where he lived, wrote, and entertained. Its name was taken from his conceit of having the inner study lined at the lintel with the portraits of thirty-six Chinese poets.

An at times overweening antiquarian concern with things Chinese was one of the marks of the *bunjin,* and here the problem of just which ones to choose consumed, it is said, half a year. Jozan closeted himself for this period in close collaboration with Hayashi Razan, one of the famous Confucian scholars of the period and long a close acquaintance.

The number chosen was established by precedent: there was a lost tenth-century anthology by Fujiwara no Kinto which had assembled a like number of Japanese poets. The actual poets chosen were argued over by the friends. Eventually they agreed and portraits—those now hanging in the room—were commissioned.

Naturally, no one knew what any of the poets had looked like and so the results were fanciful, hints of appearance being extracted from whatever poems the anonymous artist knew. All of the poets were well known by the learned Jozan, however, and it was their presence which inspired and comforted. And he wrote, as they had, in Chinese.

He wanted to be like them and in this he largely succeeded. His poem about the Chinese poet Tao Yuanming could be read as autobiography. Jozan finds him a gentleman of cultivated virtue, one who avoided success and failure alike, who was intelligent, wise and compassionate. The sage loved landscapes and in his admiration Jozan wrote that the fragrance of his love for his garden's chrysanthemums had lived after him for a whole millennium.

卍

The Shisen-do itself can be read as an illustration of these *bunjin* ideals. Not only are all thirty-six poets in place but also the oneness with nature (a *bunjin* principle) is architecturally represented.

The house opens directly onto the garden. Indeed, the structure is more a part of the garden than the other way around. The expanse of trees and bushes, sand and grass, and moss and sky comprise the doors and the windows of the Shisen-do. From the study inside, drinking tea or talking, one is also outside—a metaphor for the *bunjin* life: both a part of society and at the same time separate from it, more one with nature.

There is also, just off a corridor, a most elegant toilet. One is reminded of Tanizaki Jun'ichiro (a latter-day *bunjin*) finding it a place of placid pleasure. His example is another literary figure, the famous Natsume Soseki—novelist, essayist, poet, and the man whose face now graces the thousand-yen bill.

He, says Tanizaki, "counted his morning trips to the toilet a great pleasure, 'a physiological delight' he called it." This is because the toilet is "truly a place of spiritual repose," and, he adds, "every time I am shown to an old, dimly lit, and I would add, impeccably clean toilet in a Nara or Kyoto temple, I am impressed with the singular virtues of Japanese architecture."

Whether the dwelling was just like this in Jozan's time is something to be considered. Certainly the lower garden is much changed from then, though the upper garden with its empty space, its clipped forms, may approximate the view that the owner himself had. Hiroyuki Suzuki has written that the tradition of literati tastes truly lives in the Shisen-do. They preferred informal styles to formal, and attempted to create a spontaneous, natural appearance—in fact they also took the greatest pains to achieve this.

The verandahs, for example, are deeper than usual in order to accentuate the picture that nature makes; the round bushes on the gravel assert their nature by turning pink in the spring for these nearly abstract shapes are really azaleas; the small man-made waterfall asserts its timeless natural voice, punctuated by the rustic clatter of the *sozu*.

The latter is an ingenious contraption in which a section of cut bamboo fills with water from a streamlet until, full, it turns upon its pivot, dumps the water, and drops back upon the waiting rock with a resounding clack. Its use was originally that of an aural scarecrow—deer and boar, both destructive to gardens, were thought dispersed by the sound. At the Shisen-do, however, its role was from the first aesthetic.

It was this sound that Tanizaki Jun'ichiro's grandfather heard and so admired that he had a *sozu* made to reverberate among the storehouses and factories of Tokyo. Even now it is redolent of unspoiled forest, of pure, running water, of a natural ideal of where men actually lived which has never existed, but after which they have always hankered. The sound cleaves, the air closes, and the silence is the more deep from having been rent. Like an articulated emptiness, a space is formed by its confines.

That the place has been designated a temple (first Shingon, now Zen) intrudes not in the least. By now the vigor of Buddhism had passed. The military might and landed wealth of the temples were being destroyed and the spirit of the time was secular. Indeed, in the Tokugawa years things Buddhist were openly derided by the military aristocrats, though the common folk continued to pray.

For Jozan the Buddhist connection was slight, but it was there—largely, one thinks, because it was antique. The deity was invited in and the thirty-six immortals accommodated it, but the temple remains a home. Here in these cultivated and cultured grounds, Jozan created the illusion of a natural life. Here he lived for four decades, until his death at the age of eighty-nine, and here lives yet this embodiment of a better kind of life.

Manshu-in

 As the power of the ruling Tokugawa regime up in Edo became more apparent, the imperial court in Kyoto begin reacting against it. One of the many incidents involving shogunal authority and court indignation occurred when the emperor Go-Mizunoo bestowed honors upon a number of priests after the shogun had specifically said such was not to be done. When Edo removed the honors, Go-Mizunoo abdicated.

Only in this way, by removing himself, could an emperor now express displeasure. That, and by turning his back upon the Edo world of the shogunate and retreating into the imperial past. Following the example of Go-Mizunoo—who built himself an elegantly old-fashioned palace, the Shugaku-in, with buildings and gardens in the Heian style—the court followed, developed antiquarian tastes, and called the result Kan'ei culture, named after that short period (1624–30). This longing regard for the distant and golden past is often seen in Japanese history, perhaps because of all the destruction which this history has shown. Also, the focus of the country had moved from Kyoto, the old western capital, to the new one in the east—Edo, where now occurred nearly everything new and vital.

In Kyoto the habit of looking back upon the halcyon days of earlier times meant a regard of the golden age of the Heian period. Chinese learning came back into fashion, imperial poetry anthologies were revived, and refined avocations such as linked-verse gatherings became popular. Tea ceremony, flower arrangement, incense appreciation, were codified and revived. To have antiquarian interests was to be up-to-date. Indeed, all of our current ideas about traditional Japanese culture come from this courtly renaissance.

The best known architectural example is the Katsura Detached Villa. Deliberately rustic, it was built by Prince Toshihito and his son, Toshitada. Completed around 1640, it embodied an aristocratic nostalgia for a better time when life was simpler and more elegant. Like Marie Antoinette's Le Hameau it idealized simplicity and elevated the picturesque into an art form.

The retired Go-Mizunoo visited the place several times before constructing his own rustic retreat, the Shugaku-in. He may also have looked in at the Manshu-in which was just being constructed in 1656.

It was built by an imperial priest, Ryosho (1622–93) who was the son of a nephew of the emperor Go-Mizunoo, a member of court circles and very much up on the new aesthetic.

Its original site was located on Mount Hiei, and the original building was constructed it is said, by Saicho, the founder of Tendai Buddhism. But, though still nominally Tendai, the temple in its new site far down the mountain was not exclusively concerned with religion.

Since Buddhism was no longer a major force it could thus serve as a more or less decorative base for a display of aestheticism which gratified aristocratic nostalgia and through its ostentatious lack of ostentation, could indicate how different this court was from Edo and those upstart Tokugawas.

卐

The Manshu-in is exquisite in its evocation of an imaginary past. It is a superbly artificial container—a doll's house in which everything is scaled to a purported modesty everywhere denied by the prodigious skill with which it is put together.

Signs of this mock modesty are everywhere. The pillars are only half the width of those seen in the official architecture of the period, the thatched roof half as thick. But this apparent restraint is questioned when one considers the carpentry skill necessary to keep such a flimsy-seeming structure standing strong through the ages.

There is also, perhaps because of the distance this mountainside dwelling maintains from cozy city comfort, something slightly chilly about it. But then one remembers that Yoshida Kenko said that a house should be built with the summer in view, that in the winter one can live anywhere, but a badly built dwelling in summer is unbearable—and that the Manshu-in is designed to be

cold. Also, one recalls that coolness is often in Japan preferred and that the poet Saito Ryoku went even further when he said that elegance is frigid.

In this cabinet-like house are many rare curiosities. There is the Tiger Room with screens painted by Kano Eitoku; the Peacock Room, sliding doors painted by Ganku; the Waterfall Room, doors by Kano Tan'yu; and the Twilight Room with more pictures by Kano Tan'yu.

The garden is equally precious. Crane and tortoise islands abound, as well as a waterless waterfall (a rock) splashing out into a white sand sea. There is a magnificent espaliered pine tree which has azaleas planted beneath so that in the spring the entire tree is tinged with red.

Even now it is possible to imagine what life in this sheltered spot must have been like, surrounded by nature refined and relics from an illustrious past, resembling the retreats pictured in Beckford and Peacock, those products of the equally eclectic Gothic revival. Aiding this illusion of a cultivated leisure is a restaurant below the main gate which offers aristocratic *kaiseki:* seasonal foods—pickled fern, marinated rape, and tiny sweet river fish—all served under the autumn leaves in a most refined manner.

And just beyond the furthest hedge, there is Kyoto in the hazy distance. Sitting there one remembers that Prince Genji once looked back at Kyoto from such a height and found it like a painting, adding that people who live in such a place would hardly want to live anywhere else.

Enko-ji

 Down the hill from the elegant and secular Manshu-in sits this Zen (Rinzai sect) temple, a small white cloister with a smaller garden which attests to the modestly continuing religious role of Buddhism. It was founded in 1601 by the shogun Tokugawa Ieyasu himself, who might have had no use for emperors and their courts but who did have a use for a religion which could be turned into a means of discipline for otherwise inactive samurai.

These members of a now-idle class (the age of war over for the time being) were now to interest themselves in such arts as calligraphy and poetry, and such exercises as mock-duels. The sword, now that it was no longer to be used, became an aesthetic object to be revered. In all of this religion—particularly Zen—could assist.

Thus Ieyasu had an interest in temples, particularly small and inoffensive ones. Enko-ji, after having been moved about, as most temples eventually are, came to rest in its present location in 1667, and there it has remained, modest, unknown, dedicated to good Buddhist work.

"Where is Enko-ji?" This I asked climbing the moated paths among the hills. An old man in a new pink jogging suit pointed vaguely at a parking lot.

Over there, he said, then: "Where are you from?"

In the fall sun his bald head shone like a stone. He, lonely in his morning exercise, wanted to talk.

And so we did but he knew nothing of Enko-ji.

I persevered, however, and eventually found the entrance, modest, white, black-tiled, leaning into the customary garden of the small temple—half ornamental, half edible.

There I located the office and stood, giving my greeting, until an old woman in an apron appeared, stared, then told me that the abbess was out and indeed they were closed but added that I could look around if I wanted to.

I thanked her and thought that it was indeed somehow meaningful that I come to my last temple, the last of a long line, and found it shut, empty. *Mappo,* I reminded myself, is upon us. But I did look around.

Enko-ji has had a long and worthy history of printing Buddhist tracts and the wooden print types used are still stored there, some forty thousand in all. In addition there is the modest treasure, a thousand-armed Kannon (not on public view—she so seldom is in her more intricate manifestations) which is said to be the work of the renowned Unkei.

Since the door to the hall of the Buddha was not locked, I pushed it open and went into the incensed dark. At the altar two candles were burning and I could just make out the lacquer and the cloth of gold, shining in that dim light.

I suddenly remembered Sei Shonagon at Hase-dera and how affected she was by the Buddhist ceremony. "The lamps burned with terrifying brightness and in their light the Buddha glittered brilliantly . . . I was overcome with awe and wondered how I could have stayed away for so many months."

Here in the dim light of two candles I felt a faint stir of the emotion which had so overwhelmed her a thousand years before. Was it not, I wondered because of nature of the religion itself?

In the Western mystical experience (Judaic, Christian, Islamic) the meeting is with a personal god. Someone is standing there. In the Eastern (Hinduism, Buddhism, the religions of China), however, the mystical experience is a total and impersonal fusion. Only you are standing there. And you are facing nothing human.

卍

I imagined this small, provincial temple hall filled—filled with women. Until recently Enko-ji was a nunnery and it remains (in the large concrete building on the ground) at least in part an educational institute for nuns.

The temples of Kyoto now perform their religious function for the relatively few. (The hordes of old are still around but they now patronize Soka Gakkai and the more up-to-date beliefs.) Buddhism died and with it went the sense of religion as a part of daily life. Only in places such as Enko-ji, small,

unknown, unvisited except by the nuns and other believers, does Buddhism still play its ancient role.

Outside in the cool brilliance of an autumn noon, I walked among the bamboo surrounding little Seiryu Pond and admired the vegetables growing nearby in neat rows. So near that there was no telling if the bamboo shoot sticking a late nose from the cold ground belonged to the grove or to the garden.

And I looked out over the terraced hills, down the gentle slopes to the distant capital, hazy in the sunlit noon of late fall, and thought of those who had lived and had died in all these temples—the famous from whom I have quoted, those who had strayed into my sight, small lay-figures, and those to whom I have not given a thought and of whom I know nothing.

It is a populated landscape, these rustic palaces and provincial temples standing from the farmland, people busy in between, living in that easy proximity with the gods which is Japan's great gift.

"You find that temple?" I was asked and turned to look at the old man in the pink jogging suit, now on his way back to home and lunch.

"Yes, I did," I said.

"That's good," he said.

And just then came the stroke of an accommodating temple bell, far away, the sound dying, leaving behind its shape in the empty air.

Acknowledgments

This book has many sources. Most are indicated in the following bibliography. I owe much to these authors and their writings, though many of the ideas—particularly the more questionable ones—are my own. I am also indebted to the eminent historian, Paul Varley, who kindly read over this manuscript for me and offered thoughtful and necessary suggestions. Of these I have gratefully availed myself. The mistakes remaining are all of my own doing.

Bibliography

Agency for Cultural Affairs. *Japanese Religion: A Survey*. Kodansha International, Tokyo, 1972

Anon. *The Tale of the Heike.* (H. McCullough, trans.). Stanford University Press, Stanford, 1988

Ashihara Yoshinobu. *The Hidden Order.* (1986). Kodansha International, Tokyo, 1989

Alex, William. *Japanese Architecture.* Prentice-Hall, Int., London, 1963

Blaser, Werner. *Japanese Temples and Tea Houses.* Dodge Publishers, New York, 1956

Durston, Diane. *Old Kyoto.* Kodansha International, Tokyo, 1986

Frédéric, Louis. *Daily Life in Japan.* (1185–1603), (Eileen Lowe trans., 1972). Charles E. Tuttle, Tokyo, 1973

Fukuyama Toshio. *Heian Temples.* Weatherhill/Heibonsha, Tokyo, 1976

Futagawa Yukio. *The Roots of Japanese Architecture.* Harper & Row, New York, 1963

Guest, Harry, ed. *Traveller's Literary Companion: Japan.* Inj Print, Brighton, 1994

Hall, J./Toyoda, T. *Japan in the Muromachi Age.* University of California Press, Berkeley, 1977

Hanayama Shinsho. *A History of Japanese Buddhism.* Dendo Bukyo Kyokai, Tokyo, 1960

Hisamatsu Sen'ichi. *A Vocabulary of Japanese Literary Aesthetics.* Centre for East Asian Cultural Studies, Tokyo, 1963

Ihara Saikaku. *Koshoku Ichidai Otoko* (Life of an Amorous Man). (1682), (Kenji Hamada, trans.). Charles E. Tuttle, Tokyo, 1964

Ito Teiji. *Wabi/Sabi/Suki.* Cosmo Corporation, Tokyo, 1992

Kawabata, Y. *Koto* (The Old Capital). (J. Martin Holdman, trans., 1987). Charles E. Tuttle, Tokyo, 1988

Kamo no Chomei. *Hojoki* (The Record of a Ten-Foot-Square Hut). (Burton Watson, trans.). Shambhala Publications, Inc., Boston, 1994

Kato, Shuichi. *Japan: Spirit and Form.* (Leza Lowitz, trans.). Charles E. Tuttle, Tokyo, 1994

Keene, Donald. *Anthology of Japanese Literature.* (1955). Charles E. Tuttle, Tokyo, 1956

———. *Essays in Idleness* (*The* Tsurezuregusa of Kenko). (Donald Keene, trans., 1967). Charles E. Tuttle, Tokyo, 1981

———. *Travelers of a Hundred Ages.* Charles E. Tuttle, Tokyo, 1989

———. *World Within Walls.* Charles E. Tuttle, Tokyo, 1976

Kidder, J. Edward. *Japanese Temples.* Bijutsu-shuppansha, Tokyo, 1968

Kipling, Rudyard. *From Sea to Sea.* (1900). AMS Press, New York, 1970

Lethaby, William. *Architecture, Mysticism and Myth.* George Braziller, New York, 1975

卍 ───

Martin, John and Phyllis. *Kyoto: A Cultural Guide.* Charles E. Tuttle, Tokyo, 1994

Mishima Yukio. *Kinkaku-ji* (The Temple of the Golden Pavilion). (Ivan Morris, trans., 1959). Charles E. Tuttle, Tokyo, 1959

Morris, Ivan. *The World of the Shining Prince.* (1964). Charles E. Tuttle, Tokyo, 1978

Mosher, Gouveneur. *Kyoto: A Contemplative Guide.* Charles E. Tuttle, Tokyo, 1964

Murasaki Shikibu. *Genji Monogatari* (The Tale of Genji). (Ed Seidensticker, trans., 1976). Charles E. Tuttle, Tokyo, 1991

Paine, R.T./Soper, A. *The Art and Architecture of Japan.* (1958). Yale University Press, New Haven, 1981

Palevsky, Nick/June Kinoshita. *Gateway to Japan.* Kodansha International, Tokyo, 1990

Papinot, E. *Historical and Geographical Dictionary of Japan.* (1910). Charles E. Tuttle, Tokyo, 1972

Plutschow, Herbert E. *Historical Kyoto.* The Japan Times, Tokyo, 1983

Richie, Donald. *Kyoto Hakken* (Kyoto Rediscovered). Kodansha, Tokyo, 1981

Rimer, J. Thomas et. al. *Shisendo: Hall of the Poetry Immortals.* Weatherhill, Tokyo, 1991

Sadler, A.L. *A Short History of Japanese Architecture.* (1941). Charles E. Tuttle, Tokyo, 1962

Sansom, G.B. *Japan: A Short Cultural History.* (1931). Charles E. Tuttle, Tokyo, 1973

Sei Shonagan. *Makura no Soshi* (The Pillow Book). (Ivan Morris, trans.). Oxford University Press, New York, 1967

Slawson, David. *Secret Teaching in the Art of Japanese Gardens.* Kodansha International, Tokyo, 1987

Soper, Alexander. *The Evolution of Buddhist Architecture in Japan.* Hacker, New York, 1942

Stewart, Harold. *By the Old Walls of Kyoto.* Weatherhill, Tokyo, 1981

Tanizaki Junichiro. *In'ei Raisan* (In Praise of Shadows). (Edward Seidensticker/Thomas Harper trans., 1977). Charles E. Tuttle, Tokyo, 1984

──────. *"The Bridge of Dreams." Seven Japanese Tales.* (Howard Hibbett, trans.). Alfred A. Knopf, Inc., New York, 1963

Taut, Bruno. *Houses and People of Japan.* (1937). Sanseido, Tokyo, 1958

Toshiya Torao & Delmer Brown. *A Chronology of Japan.* Business International, Inc., Tokyo, 1987

Treib, Mark & Ron Herman. *A Guide to the Gardens of Kyoto.* Shufunotomo Co., Ltd., Tokyo, 1980

Usui Shiro. *A Pilgrim's Guide to Forty-six Temples.* Weatherhill, Tokyo, 1990

Van Wolferin, Karel. *The Enigma of Japanese Power.* (1989). Macmillan Papermac, London, 1990

Varley, Paul. *Japanese Culture: A Short History.* (1973). Charles E. Tuttle, Tokyo, 1986

Weinstein, Stanley. *Kodansha Encyopedia of Japan: Entries on various Kyoto temples.* Kodansha International, Tokyo, 1983

Yourcenar, Marguerite. *"Ah, Mon Beau Château . . . . " The Dark Brain of Piranesi and Other Esssays.* (Richard Howard, trans.). Farrar, Straus, Giroux, New York, 1984